248.4
BUR

Y0-BSW-665

Discipline That Can't Fail

Fundamentals for Christian Parents

Prov. 22:6

Dr. Arnold Burron

Third edition, 2002.

Copyright 1999 by Dr. Arnold Burron.
Originally published in 1984 by Mott Media.

Incidents and examples in this book are based upon actual occurrences. Names and selected details, where appropriate, have been changed.

MEDIA CENTER
Christian School
MARYLAND OREGON

21780

Discipline That Can't Fail

Revised 2002
Copyright 1984, 1999 by Dr. Arnold Burron

All rights reserved. Portions of this book may be reproduced *without* written permission, provided that a full citation is given, including title, author, publisher's address, and ISBN number.

Queries may be directed to the author at
phone/fax 970 330 8206, or via e-mail,
at <u>Mountainavenue@aol.com</u>

Third Edition

Cover photo by Mary Steinbacher, Photos@western-light.com

Manufactured in the United States of America

ISBN 0-9673697-1-1

This book is dedicated to the memory of my niece,
Jillian Anne Burron,
Born November 8, 1975.
Taken, unexpectedly, to be with Jesus,
June 22, 1997.

Foreword

Discipline That Can't Fail does not simply offer an encouraging word to struggling parents, it clearly details a workable plan. The author brings credibility to his claims for 100 percent success both by his personal family life, and his professional credentials. However, he is careful to point out that only in God and His Word do we have this truly "fail-safe" promise: If we do our part, God will do His part. "Our part" is attainable, but it takes hard, persistent work and requires total commitment, not only to the task, but to the divine promise that God's way does work--all the time.

In his challenging and articulate manner the author verbalizes the goal of all Christian parents and then spells out for us its inescapable implications. Surrounded as we are by the voices of self-gratification, this is a message we all need to hear. Once you have started you will not lay aside this book until it is finished. Once it is finished you will keep it close at hand for reference and review--and you will be further enriched.

One final thought: A Scripture promise the author builds on is found in Proverbs 22:6: "Train up a child in the way he should go, and when he is old he will not depart from it." The key word is *train*. The derivation of the word comes from the method Hebrew mothers used to first introduce their children to solid food. The baby was totally satisfied with mother's milk so the mother would pre-chew a basic food, then put a small amount on her finger and place it well into the child's mouth, on the palate. After several times, the child developed a taste for the new food and eagerly accepted it. The spiritual application is obvious. When from the very beginning, we develop in our children an appetite for Jesus and His Word, these tastes will form the basis for lifelong attitudes and actions. Even if one experiments with "other foods," those early tastes of childhood will always be remembered as better.

Martin Hasz, Jr.
Founder: Faith Christian Academy
Golden, Colorado

Contents

Foreword

Chapter One

Discipline: A Strange Story of Success

You probably picked this book up for one of four reasons:

1. You are apparently succeeding in administering discipline,and you're curious about whether the ideas in this book agree with what you are already doing;
2. You are apparently *not* succeeding in the discipline you've tried to provide, and you are honest enough to admit that maybe some new ideas might help;
3. You've reached the point in life at which the question of how to discipline children has become a question of key importance, and you are putting together a discipline plan.
4. Somebody gave you this book because the ideas in it seemed to be valuable, and, out of courtesy, you are looking at it.

Is This The Right Book for You?

You will find out in a hurry whether this book is for you, regardless of what your reason was for picking it up. Why? Because the whole book is based upon *one idea* about discipline. Every suggestion, every hint, every guideline, and every example points to that one main idea. If you accept the main idea, and if you work toward achieving the goal it points to, *you cannot fail* in disciplining your children.

On the other hand, if you reject the idea, and if your children do not grow up with the values that go along with the idea, your program of discipline will fail. Even if your children are well-behaved and obedient, or, if you prefer, "well disciplined", your program of discipline will fail.

Notice several things which might have been missed so far by a casual reader: The first reason listed above said that, if you picked the book up, you are *apparently* succeeding in discipline. The second reason said that you are *apparently* not succeeding. It was also asserted that, if you accept the main idea about discipline in this book, and work toward the goal it points to, *you cannot fail.* The author has no hesitation, no equivocation, no amibivalence-- absolutely no uncertainty at all--in making these assertions. Why not? Well, simply for two reasons:

1. The main idea about discipline--the basic foundation of this book--has been given to us by God Himself in the Scriptures;

2. The guarantee of success in this book, if you work and pray to achieve the main idea, also comes from God Himself.

In other words, as long as we derive our approach to discipline from the Word of God, we can confidently declare, along with Paul in 1 Corinthians 2:13, *"We speak, not in words which man's wisdom teaches, but which the Holy Ghost teaches."* And if God's wisdom teaches, and if we learn, we cannot fail.

But let's say you're a skeptic and want more objective credentials for an author besides the fact that he promises to base his or her ideas on the Bible. Even though I personally believe that other credentials are a totally insignificant part of why the principles in this book will guarantee success, some additional credentials are listed below for the skeptical reader.

First, the author holds an earned doctorate in the field of education, and worked for close to three decades as a professor at a major state university. I have taught thousands of undergraduate and graduate students, in addition to teaching in both public and private schools for ten years, including schools in rural areas as well as schools in major metropolitan areas. I have counseled literally hundreds of young people, and, based on the number of students who sent other students to me, the counseling made sense to kids and worked for them in problems ranging from drugs to abortion to shattered love relationships to hypersexuality to thoughts of suicide-- through the full range of problems facing young people today.

Perhaps an even stronger item of credibility is the fact that my wife and I have three children of our own: a daughter, nineteen; a son, eighteen; and a daughter, fourteen. Our children are not fanatics, "square," "out-of-it," naive," "do-gooders," or fanatics. They are popular with kids at school, they are enjoyed by their teachers, and they are fun for us to be around. They have proven to us again and again that children are, indeed, ". . . *an heritage of the Lord," and that ". . . they are as arrows in the hand of a mighty man." (Psalm 128:3,4).* What has become obvious to me therefore, is that the principles presented in this book have worked with my own kids, and *I am sure that I have succeeded in discipline, regardless of how my own children turn out from this point on,* for reasons I'll explain later.

A Short "P.S." to the Words Above

(It seems desirable to include these words, in parentheses, at this point. Since the paragraph above was written, during the first publication of this book in 1984, the children referred to are now grown and married, and have children of their own, and they and their spouses are raising their children according to the principles laid out in this book. I mention this here because the suggestions in this book may seem extreme to some parents, but be assured that your children will bless you, not resent you, if you follow the suggestions).

The Main Reason for Having Confidence That the Ideas in This Book Will Work for You

The ideas in this book should have at least an acceptable measure of credibility, then, even if you're a skeptic, because of the credibility of:

(1) Principles of discipline based "... *not on the words which man's wisdom teaches, but on words which the Holy Ghost teaches.*" (*1 Corinthians 2:13*).
(2) Academic and professional credentials
(3) Parental success as a disciplinarian
(4) Children, now grown, who are raising their own children the way they were raised.

Place credibility in whichever of these you will, remembering, however, that *the author claims believability only on the basis of point number one.*

Academic credentials mean nothing to me when it comes to raising children. The families of many "experts" on family issues are themselves in disarray. Good relationships with our kids and grandchildren are enjoyable, but they don't validate the message of this book. The fact that our children are raising their children the way they, themselves, were raised, also does not validate the message of this book for me. *Only the fact that what is written in this book is taken from the Word of God constitues validation.* The other reasons are listed only for people who want degrees and credentials and empirical evidence. But there's only one point of credibility which really counts: God's Word. And when

5

you rejoice in your success in providing discipline, rejoice with me in the wisdom of the Word of God in providing parents with sparklingly clear guidelines for discipline. In the end, that's all that counts.

Success in Failure: Barry's Story

Barry was the classic case of the current concept of success. At age eleven, he was identified by his teachers through a standardized testing program as a gifted child. His vocabulary was prodigious, his insights were precocious and his school achievement was superior. His brilliance was evident in Sunday school, too. Scripture texts and stories of the Old and New Testament men and women of faith were readily learned by Barry. They were remembered both at the level of immediate recall and long-term retention, even though, years later, he confided that, by age thirteen, he had begun to tacitly challenge what he was being taught in Sunday school, and that his faithful attendance and his thorough learning were a result of his parents' mandating his participation. They demanded that he attend regularly and learn thoroughly. "Church and Sunday school," he once told me, "meant nothing to me by the time I was thirteen. I heard the instructions and I learned the lessons, but I had already rejected almost everything I had been taught."

Contrary to his having to be forced to go to church and Sunday school, Barry did not have to be forced to pursue other interests, and his success was not limited to academic achievement. As a high school freshman he was a varsity football player, and as a sophomore he was a unanimous all-conference choice--one of the youngest players ever to be so honored--in the high school football league of a large metropolitan center. As his athletic fortunes rose, his personal popularity also rose. He exuded confidence and good humor, and he became one of the most sought-after students in his high school. He was the center of attention at every party, and, partly because of the naiveté of his parents, he was a participant in even the wildest activities of his peer group. He shrank from no challenge; at the time of his high school graduation he had experienced to the full, booze, drugs, and the accompanying thrills of "life in the fast lane," and had adopted a cavalier attitude about middle class morals, values, and restraints. Perhaps the exuberance and vitality of youth kept Barry from suffering the debilitating effects of his hedonistic life style, because even though athletic injuries terminated his promising athletic career, his abundant energies were channeled into academics. By the time he was twenty-one, he had graduated from college. At twenty-two, he had earned a Master's degree. At age twenty-five, he held a Ph.D. in one of the service fields, demonstrating unique talents in rehabilitating chemically dependent adults, and accepted with his usual zest an appointment to the staff of a large clinic on the west coast, where his personal and professional abilities led to his tremendous success working with hard core drug addicts. Periodic reports I received from former students who ran into Barry at professional conferences indicated that he was still popular, still successful, and still as wild as he had ever been-if not more so. One student joked that Barry ought to look eighty years old as a result

7

of his partying, "swinging," and "doping," but that he looked "as cool as he ever did."

Whether Barry had rejected God completely at this point, apparently at the pinnacle of his success, could not be readily ascertained. He simple did not think about God at all, although, if prompted, he could cite without error Scripture text upon Scripture text which he had learned half a life ago-which he did on the one occasion at which we met at a cocktail party at a professional conference-even though he would laugh derisively when he was counseled by friends with these same Scripture references attesting to God's displeasure with the decadence of his life.

It was several years after our chance meeting at the professional conference that Barry--who had seemingly vanished without leaving even a hint of his plans, re-entered my life. I was shocked to hear from him, since I had heard that not even his relatives had heard from him. As far as they knew, he was not even aware that both his parents had died, and that his family had sought diligently and vainly to contact him. The ringing of the telephone in the dark of a cold January night startled me awake. I could hear labored breathing and the telltale sound of the wires that indicated that the call was a long distance call, before I heard Barry's voice. "Doc," he said, almost in a whisper, "This is the 'Cool Dude'," referring to the affectionate nickname I had tagged on him when he was an undergraduate. I struggled to make out his next words. "I'm in trouble, " he groaned. "I've been boozin' and dopin', and I can't stop!"

Barry's call marked the first step of a geographical and spiritual journey for both of us, which began the next day in a vomit-spattered and trash-strewn room on skid row, where I found him unconscious and emaciated after making a thousand-mile journey in response to his call for help, and which would end abruptly, after many spiritual struggles and victories, with equally as little warning. Eighteen months after the midnight telephone call-after a grueling, bitter, and partially successful battle against alcohol and drugs, a rescue squad failed to revive a thirty-year-old derelict, a victim of drug and alcohol shock, on a cold sidewalk in front of a skid row flophouse.

I was not sad at Barry's funeral. I stood quietly in the shade of a huge elm tree at the cemetery, thinking back to the night just a few weeks before, when Barry had emphatically and sincerely declared, after we had talked until four in the morning, "I trust in Jesus Christ to forgive me and to give me eternal life. With the help of God, I will overcome my chemical dependence permanently. My only hope lies in God's power to help me." The fact that Barry had a "slip," or "twisted off," as it is called in the parlance peculiar to recovered alcoholics, did not alter the fact that Barry had totally and completely committed himself to the saving grace of Jesus Christ.

Who Failed?

Did Barry fail? Maybe for a short while. But despite the fact that he, like the Prodigal Son, "wasted his substance in riotous living," he, too, returned to his Father in his time of greatest need, and accepted his Father's forgiving grace. But more important to the

9

theme of this book, did Barry's *parents* fail in their attempt to provide discipline for Barry? To this question, I assert a vigorous, certain, and resounding, "NO!" Their discipline was, in fact, an unqualified success, and the reason why it was an unqualified success is the cornerstone on which the structure of this book is founded.

Chapter Two

Your Guarantee of Success

A Movie Scene to Terrify Parents

In the 1950s movie, "Fear Strikes Out," the life story of Jimmy Piersall, the professional baseball player who survived the horrors of mental illness, there is a scene in which Tony Perkins, who plays the emotionally tortured Piersall, screams a line which should be emblazoned on a plaque and given to every parent leaving a maternity ward with a new child's future in his or her hands. Perkins, his face contorted in anguish, screams in defiance to his counselors in his room in a mental institution a line embodying this sentiment: "Leave my father out of this. If it wouldn't be for my father, I wouldn't be where I am today! " At that same instant he realizes to his horror that his stirring defense of his well-meaning parent is instead a stunning indictment. He perceives that it was the unrestrained ambition of his father which contributed to his crippling emotional illness in the frenetic pursuit of "success." Child abuse, it is clear, can result even from the most well-intentioned ambition.

The Price Nobody Would Pay for Success

Do you think anybody would be willing to pay with his life if somebody would guarantee him success? You might be surprised to discover that in a survey of aspiring Olympians, over half of the young athletes stated that they would be willing to take a pill which would kill them within a year, if taking it would guarantee that they could first win a gold medal!

If there are people who are willing to die for success, what price is too high?

Let's suppose that, by some strange and mysterious process, you could guarantee that your child would become one of the following:

(1) The most valuable player in the Super Bowl, or the greatest female athlete in the world
(2) A world-renowned neurosurgeon
(3) A multimillionaire financier
(4) An internationally-recognized artist in the performing or visual arts
(5) A respected and popular world leader
(6) A famous literary or scientific figure.

Or, on second thought, suppose that you did not want your child to have the limelight and the attendant problems that go with it.

Suppose your definition of success would be that your child would enjoy good health, a good job, financial success, a beautiful home, and a happy and productive life, surrounded by a loving spouse and obedient children. Suppose further, though, that the price you would have to pay for any or all of the desirable goals listed above would be your child's eternal well-being--or, to put it another way--that the price of any desirable goal or of all of the desirable goals would be your child's loss of eternal life.

In other words, suppose you'd be required to go beyond even what the aspiring gold-medal contestants would be willing to do. Not only would *you* be willing to die if you child could attain the ideal goal you desired; you'd be willing to have *your child* lose eternal life.

So, then, it would be a simple trade: give up eternal life in heaven for success in this short life on earth.

You'd Have to be Insane to Agree to the Trade!

No sane person would even consider the payment of such a hideously exorbitant price for success. It follows, then, that there is only one logical conclusion. *By the rules of logic,* if there is nothing in the world that is worth the price of a child's eternal life, *then eternal life is more important than anything else.*

Let me repeat that, and let me go to a fresh page to do it:

> The primary, paramount, most important and immeasurably significant goal of any parent, attainable regardless of the price--including the subordination of all other goals -- worth any sacrifice, including your life or the life of your child, is your child's eternal salvation.

Great Men of the Bible Knew the Goal

Abraham:

The patriarch Abraham recognized that fact as an indisputable truth. His recognition was summed up in his willing and unhesitating obedience to God, to the extent that the physical life of his son Isaac was of little consequence when compared to the spiritual demands made by Almighty God.

Jesus, Our Savior: More Than a Man:

This same truth, that eternal life is the prize of incalculable value, exceeding in value any other goal, ambition, or aspiration is taught over and over again in the Scriptures. Jesus said, *"For what shall it profit a man if he shall gain the whole world, but lose his own soul?"* *(Mark 8:36).* And again, to reinforce the lesson that success in this world is not and should not be the goal of the Christian, Jesus told His disciples, *"Store your treasures in heaven, where they will never lose their*

14

value, and are safe from thieves. If your profits are in heaven your heart will be there too." (Matthew 6:20,21).

Paul:

The Apostle Paul, who most assuredly lived what he preached, taught the same truth. He emphatically directed the Colossians to get their values straightened out. *"Let heaven fill your thoughts,"* he declared, *"don't spend your time worrying about things down here,"* going so far as to tell them, in no uncertain terms, *"You should have as little desire for this world as a dead person does. Your real life is in heaven with Christ and God."* (Colossians 3:2,3).(TLB)

Peter:

Peter, also, in addressing the Jewish Christians who had been scattered throughout an empire sated with materialistic pleasures, anxiously exhorted them, *"Dear brothers, you are only visitors here. . ."* advising them on how to live, because their *". . . real home is in heaven."* (I Peter 2:11). (TLB)

John:

John, also, succinctly identified the emptiness of earthly goals and achievements, pointing out that the motivation for temporal success was the result of a distorted set of values. Knowing full well how ready we all are to accommodate ourselves to the society in which we live, and how we almost eagerly seize upon materialism as a way of life, John sets things straight. "Stop loving this evil world and all that it offers you," he exclaims, "for when you love these things you show that

15

you do not really love God. For all these worldly things, these evil desires-the craze for sex, the ambition to buy everything that appeals to you, and the pride that comes from wealth and importance-these are not from God. They are from this evil world itself." (I John 2:15,16).

There's No Question About It

There is absolutely no question--no room for debate of any kind--about the fact that eternal salvation is the most important goal a parent can have for his child. Since this is so, and our own logic, buttressed with the testimony of the Scriptures, renders it indisputable, then a question of monumental significance--the *most important question a parent will ever ask in his or her* life--emerges at this point.

What do I teach my children in order to be sure that they will attain eternal life in heaven?

And since the prospect of failure is absolutely terrifying; to put it bluntly, that failure means that our child will lose eternal life unless, by the grace of God, he hears the Gospel from someone else, the second most important question is,

What can I do to be *sure* that I will not fail?

The answer to the first question of *what* to teach is clear and to-the-point. It is stated with absolute clarity by the Apostle John, who writes:

And this is life eternal, that they might know thee the only true God, and Jesus Christ, whom thou has sent. (John 17:3)

And in case we miss the obvious point, it is stated again and again throughout the Old and New Testaments with different words and in different writing styles, but with the same, clear, basic theme. We must teach the Scriptures for the purpose of building faith in Christ. We must teach the Scriptures to bring about the actions which are evidence of faith in Christ. The following two sample Scriptures give us the specifics:

You know how, when you were a small child, you were taught the Holy Scriptures; and it is these that make you wise to accept God's salvation by trusting in Christ Jesus. The whole Bible was given to us by inspiration from God and is useful to teach us what is true and to make us realize what is wrong in our lives; it straightens us out and helps us do what is right. (2 Timothy 3:15,16)

Bodily exercise is all right, but spiritual exercise is much more important and is a tonic for all you do. So exercise yourself spiritually and practice being a better Christian, because that will help you not only now in this life, but in the next life too. (I Timothy 4:8)

17

Two Other Reasons That Can't be Argued Away

There is no doubt, here, on *what* we are to teach. We are to teach faith in Jesus through the Scriptures. And the process of logic has already led us to the conclusion that this is our one major task which supersedes and reduces to secondary significance all of our other tasks as parents. But if this is not enough persuasion for us, we have not only the *rules of logic* supported by informative testimony of Scripture to lead us to the inescapable conclusion regarding what our most important task is. We have also two other compellingly persuasive attestations to what we must do. The first is a direct *command* from God, in which God tells us not only *what* to do, but also *how* to do it:

And these words which I command you this day shall be upon your heart; and you shall teach them diligently to your children, and shall talk of them when you sit in your house, and when you walk by the way, and when you lie down, and when you rise. (Deuteronomy 6:6,7)

In this command, God tells us how seriously He regards our task, when He directs us to *diligently* teach our children. The word "diligently" means "without fail","systematically","consistently","seriously","earnestly"; with concentrated and deliberate effort.

Once again, our God-given logic leads us to an unavoidable conclusion. Try as we may, we cannot help but conclude that if we are to do something that must be done systematically

consistently

seriously

earnestly

with concentrated effort

deliberately,

then it is a task which must be of the most monumental significance conceivable, one which is of tremendous importance. It can only follow, logically, that if a task to be done is one of tremendous significance, performance of the task leads to tremendously significant results; conversely, failure to perform the task leads to tremendously significant consequences.

At this point, we now have two compellingly persuasive reasons to accept the fact that the best energies and abilities we have should be devoted to teaching our child those things which God says will lead to life everlasting: our own *logic*, which tells us that no material goal is worth the forfeiture of our child's soul. That logic is supported by the testimony of the Scriptures; and God's direct *command*, which tells us to get to it, to get to it thoroughly, and to get to it *now*. But there is a third reason for teaching our child the Scriptures, and the third reason is perhaps the most readily acceptableand irresistably compelling reason to regard our child's

19

salvation as our most important goal. This reason is the reason for this book. It is the reason why *we cannot fail*. This reason is a direct *promise* from God, a promise which is immutable and irrevocable:

> *Train up a child in the way he should go, and when he is old, he will not depart from it.* (*Proverbs* 22:6)

This statement by Almighty God, the Author and Finisher of our faith, is an unbreakable promise, a written guarantee of success, a guarantee that cannot be rescinded. It is a promise that, if we attend to our one, major, most significant task as parents, *we cannot fail*. Regardless of what appears to be taking place throughout our child's life as he or she grows into adulthood, such as antisocial or even worse--illegal activities, immoral behavior, personal adjustment problems, or other spiritual adversities, we do not need to fear for our child's eternal salvation if we have obeyed God and followed His command. If we have "trained our child in the way he should go," God does not say:

"it is *likely* that when he is old he will not depart from it,"

or

"it is *probable* that when he is old he will not depart from it,"

or

"*chances are,* there's a statistically significant tendency that. . ." or even that it is *desirable* to train a child, because it "enhances the possibilities that he may someday reflect his early training," or some other platitudinous empty conjecture.

God says that if we train him up in the way he should go, when he is old *HE WILL NOT DEPART FROM IT!* Think of it! Guaranteed success. We need only do as God commands-systematically, seriously, purposefully, and consistently. And God provides further assurance that, as we and our children follow the leading of the Holy Spirit, we will succeed. Proof of this fact encourages us again and again in the Scriptures, for despite the fact that we are warned to "be vigilant," and to steep ourselves in the Word of God to resist the relentless onslaught of the Evil One, God says:

He which hath begun a good work in you will continue it until the day of Jesus Christ (Philippians 1:6),
and that
. . .it is God who worketh in us both to will and to do that which is His good pleasure. (Philippians 2:13)

The Scriptures provide other statements of God's encouragement, stating that it is God

Who shall confirm you unto the end, that ye may be blameless in the day of our Lord Jesus Christ. (I Corinthians 1:8)

And again that,

My sheep hear my voice, and I know them and they follow me; and I give unto them eternal life, and they shall never perish, and no one shall snatch them out of my hand. (John 10:27,28)

21

If we obey God, we are carefully and with the guidance and help of the Holy Spirit, building a foundation for our child which is based on the Word of God; a foundation of which Jesus Christ Himself says:

All who listen to My instructions and follow them are wise, like a man who builds his house on solid rock. Though the rain comes in torrents, and floods rise and the storm winds beat against his house, it won't collapse, for it is built on rock." (Matthew 7:24,25 TLB)

Thus, no "rain," no "wind," nor any other tempestuous adversities in life--no circumstances at all, singly or in combination--can destroy what has been built for our children if we build our program of training and discipline on the Word of God, according to the instructions of God. We are totally confident that we cannot fail in carrying out our responsibilities in providing discipline, for we believe God when He says,

"In the fear of the Lord one has strong confidence, and his children will have a refuge." (Proverbs 14:26).

In the final analysis, this is the only definition of *success* that matters to Christian parents.

Yes, But What About So-and-So's Kids?

There are theologians who argue that what God says, here, in Proverbs, is not a promise. They claim that it is a general statement which expresses a sentiment that is usually true. In other words, they claim, the proverb merely says that, generally speaking, children will usually do in older age what, as children, they were trained to do.

Other theologians assert that the verse means that, if we train up a child according to his natural inclinations, when he is old he will adhere to that training. The Amplified Bible seems to follow this line of thinking. But the Amplified Bible includes, in its cross-references, II Timothy 3:15. That verse supports the "promise" interpretation of Proverbs 22:6.

What seems to be the problem when theologians wrestle with how to interpret Proverbs 22:6 is pretty easy to see. Those who say that the verse is not a promise seem to be trying to explain an anomaly: a child who has gone the wrong way, even though his parents have "brought him up right." We can all cite an example of a situation where parents seemed to have "done everything" for their children, and yet, their children "went wrong", or "turned out wrong." Let's face it--it's difficult to explain how parents who seemed to do everything right ended up with kids who seemed to do everything wrong. But trying to reconcile that paradox by suggesting that Proverbs 22:6 is talking about being sensitive to a child's natural "bent" or "inclinations", or, as contemporary educators would say, "learning style", is not a reasonable interpretation. After all, if a child is "naturally inclined" in a certain direction, he will go that direction. You don't have to train a child to go in a direction he was headed toward in the first place! If, as it has been argued, it is "his nature" to go a certain way, he'll go that way. Something so obvious and mundane would hardly qualify to be included in one of the Bible's "Wisdom Books" of profound insights and directives.

But there's also something else wrong with the claim that the verse is merely telling us to train up a child according to his natural inclinations. Those who hold that interpretation do so despite the fact that much of the Book of Proverbs is made up of promises. We continually read, "If this--then this." Promises are both explicitly stated and inescapably inferred from beginning to end in the Book of Proverbs. Further, the Book of Proverbs has many specific instructions for young people, promising them that, *if* they heed the instructions of their parents, *then* . . . and there is a promise of the good things which will follow.

More on interpretations later. (Appendix B in this book has an in-depth discussion on interpretation, and on why the position of this book is that Proverbs 22:6 is, indeed, a promise.) It is also the position of this book that God has provided specific guidelines for us which we can follow in complete confidence.

In summary, as a result of

    (a) logic
    (b) the testimony of Scripture
    (c) God's commandment and promise

we know the following things:

The Main Ideas That Are the Foundation of This Book

(1) We know that our most important goal is to provide the conditions necessary to build faith in Christ.

(2) We know that to do this we must teach the Scriptures.

(3) We know that God commands us to use our best efforts to*diligently* teach our children.

(4) We know that God promises that if we obey His commandment, our children, when they are old, will not depart from what we have taught them.

(5) We know that it is *not* up to us to create faith in our child. That's the Holy Spirit's responsibility. Our responsibility is to provide the best conditions necessary within which the Holy Spirit can work. Creating and sustaining faith is *His* task. Thus, we know that, with the help of the Holy Spirit, we cannot fail.

Chapter Three

Back To The Basics:
The Biggest Mistake
Parents Make

Each fall in the rugged Rocky Mountains of Colorado, thousands of hunters take to the high country to wander jeep trails, logging roads, and pristine pine forests in pursuit of deer and elk. For most hunters, the hunt is satisfying whether or not they are successful in bagging game; the alluring beauty of the seemingly unending forests, the crystal clear mountain streams, and the persistent whispering of the wind in the trees have an effect on a hunter which refreshes and recharges him, and which is a calming tonic for weeks afterward as he faces the demands of urban living.

For some hunters, though, who embark on the hunt unprepared, the mountains become a malevolent, life-threatening, terrifying evil. In the space of an hour, the sunny grove of aspen trees in the pleasant meadow changes dramatically. The comforting sunlight and the soft caress of an Indian Summer breeze can become a frigid arctic nightmare of twisted and splintered tree trunks, drifting snow, and screaming winds.

Suddenly the friendly and familiar jeep trails and logging roads are buried, the pristine peaks are swallowed up in a madness of white, the whisper of the soft breeze turns into the raging fury of a mountain blizzard. The mountains, with frightening swiftness, become menacing. Their power is overwhelming, and the unwary hunters, who, just a few short hours before could not even begin to imagine the swirling terror engulfing them, become disoriented, lost, bewildered, and terrified. Each year the result for some inexperienced or unprepared hunters is death. On more than one occasion the author has watched incredulously a beginner refuse to take seriously the warnings of experienced companions. The unsuspecting novice will wander off into Forest Service land designated as "Wilderness Area," clad only in light clothing and tennis shoes, carrying no matches, compass, or other survival gear, blithely assuming that the picnic-like, eighty-degree autumn weather will obligingly stay that way until he finishes his excursion. And frequently, disbelief and inexperience exact a painful lesson, resulting in an eleventh-hour rescue by a mountain search and rescue team.

The Most Competent Are Also The Most Careful

It seems to be a strange paradox that the most competent hunters are also the most cautious. The author has observed experienced hunters embarking on a hunt carrying backpacks containing survival gear, emergency rations, first aid supplies, and other equipment necessary for successfully meeting any contingency. These hunters know the territory, but they nevertheless check their compasses before starting out. They periodically meet to check on one another. They carry down-filled coats and all-weather clothing in their thirty-pound packs even in eighty-degree weather, knowing that the pack will make canyon climbing tougher and the hunt more rigorous. But they are willing to take on the task of carrying the contingency equipment because they know that what is seemingly the most friendly and benign haven from the stresses of city life can become the most forbidding and furious foe. In short, they survive because they are prepared to survive. And they are prepared to survive for two reasons: first of all, though they do not fear the mountains, they respect them; and secondly, which is perhaps the more important reason, they take the mountains seriously.

Life Seems Like a Friendly Meadow--But Our Kids Are Traveling Through A Wilderness

In much the same way, the environment in which we and our children pursue successful completion of our daily affairs seems to be a benign and relatively safe environment. True, we are faced with challenges and temptations, but, we think, we seem to be doing all right. And, like the inexperienced neophyte mountaineer, we blithely send our children off to pursue the hunt for success in school, in sports, or in other social settings. Particularly in the free world, where terrorism, famine, war, and pestilence seem to be only as frightening as the blizzard one reads about in a novel while curled up in a chair next to a crackling fireplace, we are lulled into complacency. The external trappings of safety--good food, adequate shelter, competent health care, professional emergency systems--an aura of well-being, lull us into what might be called "benign neglect." We are mesmerized into some hypnotic state of assuming that everything is just fine. We simply fail to realize that, while everything appears to be well, our material blessings in many ways can be a curse, for we become, as the Scripture says, "blind fools," totally unprepared for the violent forces which at any moment could engulf us and destroy us. While we stroll through what seems to be a picnic ground in a golden grove of autumn aspen, a massive storm front surrounds us. Things seem to be pretty good, and most of the time we have a calm sense of well-being. But God presents us with an entirely different set of facts. And what He tells us ought to make us as alert as we would be if we heard a news report that a psychotic child killer was stalking our neighborhood, looking for his next victim!

A Psychotic Child-Killer--In Our Homes!

At this point, if this sounds like an attempt to terrify you, read on, because you're "right on." The biggest mistake many of us make in raising and disciplining our children is that many of us haven't taken the job as seriously as we should have. Not only have we not planned our campaign, we haven't even recognized our enemy. Worse than that, *most parents have not consciously thought about the fact that there is an enemy!* We've disciplined our kids to make them "behave properly"-whatever that is-usually when some undesirable behavior has come up. We've used whatever techniques seemed appropriate at the moment. We haven't thought about the *goal* of effective discipline, described in the preceding chapter. We haven't done any of these things because we're not scared enough. And yet God tells us that the psychotic child killer is not only lurking in our neighborhood-he's hiding in our house! Listen to this:

For we are not fighting against people made of flesh and blood, but against persons without bodies--the evil rulers of the unseen world, those mighty satanic beings and great evil princes of darkness who rule this world; and against huge numbers of wicked spirits in the spirit world. (Ephesians 6:12 TLB)

Now, is this a tough enemy? Well, let's examine the words used to describe what we're fighting against:

evil rulers
mighty satanic beings
great evil princes of darkness
huge numbers of wicked spirits

This enemy is so terrible, says the Apostle Jude, that even Michael, one of the mightiest of the angels, when he was arguing with Satan "... *did not dare to accuse Satan, or jeer at him, but simply said, 'The Lord rebuke you'."* (Jude 1:9). Michael did not even dare to take Satan on one-to-one, even verbally! Plainly, we are up against an enemy so overwhelmingly powerful that the writers of Scripture virtually exhausted their powers of description as they tried to convey to us the intensity of the forces of evil threatening to destroy us.

Now, just what is this treacherous and ruthless enemy up to? Does he merely meander around, contenting himself with initiating a quarrel here, a conflict there? Does he, maybe, on his more successful days, wreak enough havoc to create the climate for a few sensationalistic crimes, striving all the while to instigate a few wars, holocausts, or mass murders?

God tells us that what Satan does is of exceedingly greater consequence than Satan's afflicting us with such tribulations and troubles. For we can and will overcome problems which are common to all mankind. For example, if a criminal were to assault us, we would eventually recover from the assault. If a thief stole from us, we would recover from that, too. If we are victimized by war, terrorism, poverty, or disease, Jesus tells us not to be afraid. He says, *"Fear not them which kill the body, but are not able to kill the soul, but rather, fear Him who is able to destroy both soul and body in hell"* (Matthew 10:28).

Scripture tells us that such problems caused by Satan here on earth should not be our primary concern. God tells us what our enemy is really up to. In Peter's First Epistle, God warns us:

*Be sober, be vigilant, for your adversary, the
devil, walketh about as a roaring lion, seeking
whom he may devour. (I Peter 5:8)*

So this is our *adversary.* Our *enemy.* Our *opponent.*
Our *foe.* And his goal? Our complete, absolute, utter
destruction! And one of the most powerful weapons in
his arsenal is that he is the "father of lies."

"Nowadays"--The Catch-All of All Excuses

Satan can be hypnotically and compellingly
persuasive. What he says sounds good. In fact, regardless
of the era in which he has operated, what he has said has
always fit in with "the times." After all, haven't you heard
people start a sentence with the word, *"Nowadays. . ."* and
then go on to tell why it has become commonplace to
ignore this or that unacceptable behavior which, in the
past, would have totally violated even the most loosely-
defined parameters of decency or acceptability? And the
astounding thing is that we repeatedly believe our enemy!
Our credulity is stretched to the point of infantile
gullibility, but we still swallow Satan's lies with ease. We
forget that Jesus warned us that *"in the last days, false
prophets shall appear, and lead many astray. Sin will be
rampant everywhere, and will cool the love of many"*
(Matthew 24:11,12). *"When I return the world will be as*

32

indifferent to things of God as the people were in Noah's day" (Luke 17:26 TLB). So we listen to the father of lies, about whom Jesus says, in John 8:44, *"...there is not an iota of truth in him."* But we listen anyway. And we get some ideas which sound okay to us. And we become understanding." And "accepting." And "realistic." And "tolerant" of ideas and behaviors which would make even a jackal puke in disgust. But we think we should be "accepting" and "tolerant" and "understanding" and "realistic" because, after all,

"Nowadays . . . "

What kind of ideas do our kids get "nowadays?" Well, I've heard my college students laughingly describe one of their friends who got "blitzed," deriving great amusement over how he or she sat on the floor, chin resting on the rim of the toilet bowl, retching bile as a result of vomiting to the point of reaching the "dry heaves," trying to throw up booze. God says, *"Wine is a mocker, strong drink is raging, and whosoever is deceived thereby is not wise,"* *(Proverbs 20: 1)* and that the one who has the bitterest of sorrow is the person whose will and personality have been captured and victimized by alcohol *(Proverbs 23:29,35).* But now it's "cool" to describe half-conscious, drunken vomiting into the toilet as "kissing the porcelain queen," or "topping the porcelain pizza," when a young person is so drunk that he or she has to sit on the floor, hanging onto the toilet bowl for support, puking his insides out. I have also heard how "neat" it is to sleep with someone because the ultimate act of kindness is to share one's body with someone who has "needs."

Other Lies That Pass for Truth

There are some other popular lies that have been around for years, like the one about how self-denial is harmful--how pent-up emotions and frustrated desires can be detrimental, and how they can cause all sorts of psychiatric problems. Devotees of this set of lies have bestowed upon us the gift of therapy involving the technique of "primal screaming," where people sit and scream, at the top of their lungs like a tribe of tormented and agitated baboons in some tropical rain forest, in order to rid themselves of inhibited frustration."Nowadays," begins the verbalization of another "reasonable sounding" lie, we should be "assertive." We shouldn't deny ourselves the fulfilling of our own desires and conveniences. We should not hold back our hostility, because the "stress" of self-denial and "bottling up" of hostility will make us sick. I've also heard these next ones so many times that they stick, like some genius advertising man's jingle, in my mind: "As long as it doesn't hurt anybody else, if it seems right and you feel good about it, do it. You have to grow," and, "We're not supposed to be judgmental." The last time I heard these lines, though, I realized how convoluted and perverted this line of reasoning had become. A young coed, who offered it as her excuse for sleeping with a man almost thirty years her senior, with the full consent of his wife, ventured the opinion that it was perfectly okay, because the wife felt that, "Nowadays" a wife should give her mate the freedom of an "open marriage" so that "needs" could be met. Indeed, a variation of that lie was asserted

34

in the Presidential Scandal of 1999, in which the president's partner in perfidy ventured that her adultery with the president was merely her attempt to provide him with contact with "the real world"--a contribution, to be sure, that she felt was not generally recognized, and, in fact, undervalued now that the truth was known.

It is now healthy to "do your own thing" and to "go for it." "Whatever turns you on!" is the cocky clarion call rallying the "Me" generation to action. It doesn't matter, "nowadays," that Jesus says:

Anyone who wants to follow Me must put aside his own desires and conveniences and carry his cross with him every day and keep close to me. (Luke 9:23 TLB)

It is totally insignificant "nowadays" that Jesus says that, instead of giving vent to hostility, anger, and aggression, and instead of practicing "assertiveness" to protect and insist upon our rights,

Don't resist violence! If you are slapped on one cheek turn the other too. (Matthew 5:39 TLB)

"Nowadays," it is not relevant to the values of the world that Jesus says,

If someone demands your coat, give him your shirt besides, (Luke 6:29 TLB) and that if we are compelled to walk one mile, we should willingly go the extra mile. *(Matthew 5:41).*

35

Current concepts of morality, ethics, and acceptable social behavior, carefully disguised in the garb of "good mental health," "honesty," and other high-sounding terminology show that the "father of lies," Satan, has greater credibility in our children's schools, their entertainment, and their total developmental environment than the teachings of the Son of God. All the lies and distortions of the truth sound *so good*. They are just--"y'know--right." But God says,

There is a way that seems right to a man, but the end thereof is DEATH! (Proverbs 14:12)

There is no doubt that God is by no means talking about physical death. He is telling us that man has an obstinate and stubborn desire to create his own value system, and to make it sound so good that is seems unarguably logical, reasonable, considerate of others, sensible, and "right." But God tells us that if our children are allowed to follow this right-sounding and intellectually-appealing value system, they will DIE. They will suffer the anguish of the loss of their eternal souls!

What Would You Do If You Saw This Happen?

The next time you look with love and admiration at your children's school portrait photographs, imagine this scene. Imagine the most beguiling, kind-looking stranger sitting in your home, quietly talking to you in lighthearted and carefree conversation, making you feel good, and leading you to delight in the adroitness of your own social skills and your own ability to entertain. Imagine that same visitor, in the midst of the titillating conversation, walking over to the television set or the bookshelf or wherever you display your children's school photographs. Visualize this stranger reaching out, taking in hand, and examining a photograph of one of your children. Then, imagine that, while he is still trying to distract you with fascinating and amusing conversation, he flings the picture to the floor, shattering the glass into a hundred shards, grinding his heel into the happy, innocent face on the picture. Then, imagine the stranger snatching the mutilated photograph from the floor, and tearing and shredding the smiling face into tatters. You would be uncontrollably infuriated and outraged; after your initial stunned shock, you would leap into action to bodily throw the person out of your house! There is no way on earth that you would ever have knowingly allowed anyone with such perverse and vile intentions into your home.

The Worst Child-Molester of All

Dear parent, what the father of lies, the enemy, intends to do is *exactly* what has just been described. But not to your child's picture. To your child!

If what you've read so far sounds like extremism, close the book. It is extremism, and the rest of the suggestions in this book are equally as extremist. However, if you are ready to take the job of discipline

MEDIA CENTER
Christian School
PORTLAND, OREGON

seriously, read on. You and I will be "on the same page", and we'll move forward together.

If the Holy Spirit has convinced you--as he has convinced me beyond a flicker of a doubt--that your child's discipline is the most important task you'll ever have, then the next chapters are for you. Obviously, you are ready to make a sincere commitment to the serious job of providing God-pleasing discipline for your child. You realize, as I do, that the biggest mistake most parents make is their failure to take the task of discipline seriously, because they fail to understand Satan's threat to their children. You are prepared to do your best to do what *has to be done* , which is the subject of the rest of this book.

Chapter Four

What *Must* I Do
To Succeed In Discipline?

Let's say that you are convinced that what God says is true. If we make a list of the things God says--and remember, the only thing that this book has done so far *is to restate what God says,* not what authorities in child development, or pedagogues, or psychologists say--we'd list these points:

(1)   If we "Train up a child in the way he should go, when he is old, he will not depart from it."

(2)   This "training in the way he should go"--our primary goal, the goal which supercedes all other goals, the goal we would die for--is to lead our child to eternal life.

(3)   We are in combat with a deadly and awesomely powerful enemy. Our enemy's goal is to utterly annihilate and destroy our children.

"Did"--Not "Should"--is What Counts

The thought which comes up next, then, might be this question: *What,* exactly, should I do? But we are not at all interested in what *we should* do, or what we *intend* to do. It is not without some validity that there is an old saying which has endured for generations, which says, "The road to hell is paved with good intentions." Case after case can be cited where well-intentioned people said, "We should . . .," and you can complete the sentence with whatever ending you like, knowing full well that the action was never carried out. Let me give you a few examples:

Doris, a young mother of two preschoolers, traveled to Cheyenne, Wyoming, a one-hundred-mile trip from her home in Denver, to pick up her three-year-old daughter, Amy, who was visiting Grandmother. Doris took along Amy's baby-sitter, to help take care of Amy and Amy's two-year-old brother, Billy, on the way home. Amy, who was Grandma's only granddaughter, was naturally reluctant to leave Grandma's house to return home, for her every whim had been responded to with an alacrity that only a doting grandparent can provide. Her reluctance quickly took the form of obstinate uncooperativeness, and she began a shrieking session which persevered from Grandma's kitchen through the outskirts of Cheyenne, and which became an unbearable display of temper, stubbornness, and whining by the time her mother had driven thirty miles south on the highway to Denver. Fortunately, at that point on the highway, an exit ramp was available, and Doris could now have the opportunity to remediate the situation. And remediate the situation she did. "I couldn't believe it!" exclaimed her shocked baby sitter, a college student of mine. "The child was screaming, kicking at her mother, and totally ignoring my attempts to distract her. The mother went up the exit ramp, across the overpass, down the ramp on the other side, and back to grandmother's house, where grandma, undaunted by Amy's disobedience, served as a willing accomplice in extending Amy's visit for another day or two, until Amy felt more "settled" about leaving.

Doris certainly taught Amy a lesson. She taught not only Amy, but she taught Billy, also. But what did Doris teach? Doris taught:

Selfishness
Lack of consideration
Unrestrained temper
Disobedience
Obstinacy
Self-centeredness

Why did she teach this? It was *inconvenient* to take the time to take corrective action. It was *bothersome* to provide an appropriate response. It was *difficult* to correct Amy's behavior. It was *unpleasant* to do what had to be done. In other words, the bottom line was that the parent put her own needs before the child's needs! Doris had a need for what was convenient and stress-free. Doris was not so obtuse that she did not realize the impression she was making on the baby-sitter. "I *should* give Amy a good spanking," Doris told my student. "I *should* teach her that this behavior is totally unacceptable, " she offered. "I *should* have a talk with her grandmother about how she *should* respond to Amy during their visits," she confessed to the sitter. Doris, it was clear, knew very well what *should* have been done.

Another example is Max. His fifteen-year-old son wanted to attend an unchaperoned party where beer and wine would be available. Max didn't feel good about the situation, but after all, Jerry *did* ask permission to go, and he *did* tell Max that beer and wine would be available, and he *did* request permission to drink. Max told me, "I know that I probably *should* tell Jerry that he can't go. I'm not comfortable with the idea of a lot of kids at the party who I don't know. But I don't want Jerry to be the only one in his class who can't go." Susan, Max's wife, volunteered the suggestion that Max *should* call the host parents to find out whether they knew about and approved of the beer and wine. "And," Susan added, "you probably *should* find out who the kids are who will be at the party, and then you *should* call their parents to find out whether they know about the beer and wine." In private, Susan confided, "I *should* just insist that Jerry stay home, because I don't approve of this at all, but Max thinks Jerry should be allowed to go, and frankly I just don't feel like having another hassle with Jerry and Max both ganging up on me."

Let's count the "shoulds" here:

Max *should* tell Jerry that he can't go.
Max *should* call the host parents.
Max *should* find out who the other kids are.
Max *should* call the other parents.
Susan *should* insist that Jerry stay home.

Score: *Shoulds* = 5
Dids = 0

Jerry went to the party. Jerry drank booze. Jerry "got off" on the booze. The party was wilder than usual. Everybody was "laid back." Jerry can't wait to go to the next party. And it doesn't take a creative imagination to describe the scenario at successive parties as Jerry grows into young adulthood. If Jerry is fortunate, he'll survive the emotional and physical pitfalls of his parent-tolerated adolescent pursuits. If not, he'll experience what Joyce experienced.

Another Shutout

Joyce is a girl who frequented the neighborhood community center in a suburb in which I once lived. I saw Joyce only twice in the four years after I moved across town. Once was at a Fourth of July parade, and, although I had not known her much beyond recognizing her as a familiar face at the community center, and saying "hi" to her and her mother, she was still immediately recognizable as the neighborhood kid who had participated in the recreational activities at the community center four years before.

The second time I saw Joyce, I didn't recognize her immediately. I was out jogging on a country road on the outskirts of town one night when I heard, around a bend ahead of me, the screeching of rubber on concrete, followed by the explosive sound of breaking glass and collapsing steel. Racing to the scene, I found an automobile which was a total loss. Near the car, a teenage girl was lying in a cornfield. She had apparently gone through the windshield. Another girl, in shock, was kneeling beside her. Their car had left the road, caromed off a telephone pole, and plowed into the stubble of the cornfield. The girl lying on the ground was throwing up what looked like blood. I turned her on her side so she wouldn't drown in it. I was positive that she was suffering a massive internal hemorrhage, and that she was in extremely critical condition. Then I smelled it. Port wine! The sixteen-year-old lying in a stupor on the cold ground in a stubble-and-snow-covered cornfield was vomiting wine! And as I became conscious of the other teenager kneeling in the snow across from me, I caught a glimpse of her face in the glare of the spotlight of the ambulance. It was Joyce.

It took over two hours to locate Joyce's parents. They were at a party. They had gone out apparently not knowing where Joyce would be that night, without knowing who she was going with, without knowing what she would be doing, without knowing when she would be getting home, and without knowing the conditions under which she would be driving. And so Joyce went out, drank a liberal supply of port, partied with her friends, missed a curve in the road, demolished her parents' car, and nearly killed herself and her friend. Without doubt, Joyce's parents counted some "shoulds" that would have been appropriate. "We *should* have asked Joyce what her plans were for the evening, and we *should* have given Joyce some instructions on what we expected of her while we were gone," were probably some painful thoughts they had on their way home. Joyce's mother told me later, in a mood of deep reflection, "We *should* teach Joyce a lesson. I think we *should* ground her for awhile."

44

Did mom and dad "ground" Joyce? Within a month, the insurance company money bought a new car. An economy car. "Because Joyce does a lot of driving," her mother cheerfully explained, "and it'll help us save on gas."

Score: *"Shoulds"* = 4
"Dids" = 0

Another shutout. Another loss.

It doesn't seem necessary here to list the negative lessons Joyce learned. Both Joyce's and Jerry's parents probably had a lot of seemingly reasonable excuses for not doing what they should have done. Hassle. Conflict. Inconvenience. They clearly knew what they *should* have done; nevertheless they did *not* do it.

You will never be sorry for doing what you MUST do. Remember Cassie Bernal? She was the 17-year-old who was shot to death by a maniacal classmate in the Colorado high school massacre of early 1999. "Yes, I do!" she unflinchingly replied when her murderer demanded to know whether she believed in God. Millions of people were inspired by Cassie Bernal's faith.

Few are aware, however, that only two years before, she had dabbled in witchcraft and was fascinated with suicide. But Cassie's parents had done what they knew they *must* do: ignoring her protests, they moved her to a different school, grounded her from all activity and contact except a church youth group, and diligently monitored her activities. Imagine the comfort they have now! They know that they did what *had* to be done.

Imagine their regret if they were able to wail only a remorseful, "We *should* have . . ."!

45

It is clear that "What *should* I do?" is not a relevant question for parents who are serious about their child's eternal life. Like the jailer in Acts 16:30, who fell on his knees before Paul and Silas, earnestly imploring, "Sirs, what *must* I do to be saved?" the only relevant question for parents who realize that discipline is a deadly serious responsibility, is the question, "What *MUST* I do?"

Must Number One

Few things frustrate me more as a university professor and a confidant of young people than to see kids groping in every direction, seeking even a sliver of light at the end of their psychological tunnels, when the answer is right in front of them. One typical example is Sarah. She spent large amounts of time, money, and energy, trying to find "balance." First she tried a biofeedback workshop. That didn't tell her why she felt empty and why life seemed meaningless. I tried to tell her about Jesus. She looked at me like I had plague. Nevertheless, she was soon back again. She was now trying sexual freedom, but, she admitted, she still felt empty. Once again, I tried to share Jesus. Still the plague. On Sarah's next "drop in," a few weeks later, she told me about her human sensitivity class in the "open university" run by students.

"Was it providing fulfillment?" I wondered.

"No, but it's neat," Sarah responded, and with pot-glazed eyes and in hushed, almost secretive tones, she ventured that it was helping her find her "center," whatever that was. On Sarah's last visit to my office, she was soliciting donations to attend a retreat in the mountains to pursue "spiritual oneness" through some new meditative therapy whose name at the moment escapes me, much as elusive happiness and fulfillment continue to escape Sarah. Sarah will be dropping by my office again. I'm positive of that. She'll still be trying to "get it together." And she'll have another head trip to tell me about. But as long as she fails to look at the Word of God, I am convinced that she will fail to find the peace she is looking for.

Sarah--and more of my young friends like her than I care to count--stretch my capacity to understand. They absolutely refuse to look at the Word of God, because they have no inkling of the fantastic power available to them. And when I see posters around the university campus advertising this or that "new" solution or new guru, and then watch the Sarahs of the world follow each one in turn without finding peace, I am reminded of what Jesus said about those who construct elaborate, man-made spiritual philosophies which are not based on the Word of God:

> *They are blind guides leading the blind, and both will fall into a ditch. (Matthew 15:14 TLB)*

Parenting Power: There for the Taking

Sadly, Jesus' words apply to discipline, too. Maybe you thought, as you began this section of the chapter, that you'd immediately find a list of *musts* for our children. But the first *must* is not for our children. The first *must* is for parents.

The Apostle Paul, in writing to his Christian friends in Ephesus whose "strong faith" he rejoices in and commends them for, nevertheless still says to them, *"I pray that you will begin to understand how incredibly great His power is to help those who believe Him"* (Ephesians 1:19).(TLB)

Notice that he is praying that these Christians, Christians of "strong faith," will *begin* to understand. In other words, they hardly have a clue--almost no idea at all--about God's power, which Paul says is *incredibly great. Unbelievably* great! Paul realizes that, if these people even *begin* to understand, they will unleash dynamic and powerful forces of faith that will totally, completely, and overwhelmingly change their lives!

Tragically, one of the reasons why people do not even begin to understand how incredibly great God's power is to help those who believe Him is that they, like Sarah and countless others, have not even the tiniest concept of the tremendous power of the Word of God, choosing instead, as Paul says in Romans 1:21 (TLB), *". . . to think up silly ideas of what God was like and what He wanted them to do."* Likewise, millions of parents--even Christian parents--do not even come close to the success they could have in providing discipline, because they do not even *begin* to understand the incredibly fantastic power of the Word of God. If they did even *begin* to understand the power of the Word of God, *this understanding alone would change their methods of discipline more than any other understanding or knowledge they could ever acquire.*

At this point, it's really quite easy to see what the first *must* is in providing discipline that can't fail. It isn't

48

a *must* which we do to our kids. It is a must which we absolutely have to have for ourselves. The first *must* in a step-by-step program of discipline that can't fail is that *we must be aware of the incredible power of the Word of God.*

Now, what kind of power are we talking about? Most of us know the Scripture reference of the mustard seed. Or at least we think we do. Nine out of ten Christians, when asked about this reference, answer by alluding to the Scripture text which talks about being able to move mountains if we have faith equivalent in size to a grain of mustard seed. But there is another reference, a parable, which teaches us that the mustard seed *"... is the smallest of all seeds, but becomes the largest of plants, and grows into a tree where birds can come and find shelter"* (Matthew 13:32). (TLB) The point of this parable is also made in Jesus' references to salt, yeast, and light; namely, that even what seems to be the most insignificant witness to others about God's Word has unbelievable capacity for growth and development, producing a yield far beyond our expectations. The Bible says:

"For whatever God says to us is full of living power: it is sharper than the sharpest dagger, cutting swift and deep into our innermost thoughts and desires with all their parts, exposing us for what we really are." (Hebrews 4:12 TLB)

God also provides further evidence of the dynamic power of His Word, when He tells us in 2 Peter 1: 19:

"... You will do well to pay close attention to everything (the prophets) have written, for, like lights shining into dark corners, their words help us to understand many things that would otherwise be dark and difficult. But when you consider the wonderful truth of the prophets' words, then the light will dawn in your souls and Christ the Morning Star will shine in your hearts. (TLB)"

So the Word of God *changes things*.

It changes situations.
It changes attitudes.
It changes personalities.
It changes people.
It changes behaviors.

The startlingly undeniable truth is that the Word of God is the *chief agent* for changing lives! It has incredibly great power for parents in carrying out a program of discipline that can't fail because as parents grow in their knowledge and fear of God, the Word of God will do these things for parents:

(1) Create strong confidence (Proverbs 14:26)
(2) Provide insight (Proverbs 9:10)
(3) Lead to prosperity and happiness
      (Proverbs 16:20)
(4) Offer security and a refuge (Proverbs 30:5)
(5) Point out the right path to follow
      (Psalm 119:105)
(6) Lead parents to glow with Christ's power
      (Peter I:19)

(7) Refresh them, make them wise, enlighten
their judgment, and keep them in good
spirits (Psalm 19:7,8)

What the Word Will Do For Children

The Word of God also has incredibly great power for children in a program of discipline that can't fail, because it will do these things for children:

(1)   Make children wise to accept God's salvation (2 Tim.3:15).

One could conclude the list right there, because that is the ultimate goal of all God-pleasing discipline, but there are more things that the Word of God can do for children:

(2)   Children will be kept and guarded by the Word (Proverbs 4:6).
(3)   Knowledge of God will provide insight (Proverbs 9:10).
(4)   Children will be preserved from evil, they will be led to walk in the right paths, and will develop patterns of thinking which will guide their actions (Proverbs 6:20-23; Psalm 119:105).
(5)   Children will be followers of Jesus Christ. They will not have guilt-trips, hang-ups, or unfulfilled needs to find spiritual peace, because they "will know the Truth, and the Truth will make them free" (John 8:32).

In Chapter Two of this book, we used logic to arrive at the indisputable conclusion that the most important goal of any parent is his or her child's eternal salvation.

Our God-given logic leads us, at this point, to another vitally significant fact:

The first *must* in a program of discipline that can't fail is that we *must* recognize the tremendous power available to us in the Word of God. Therefore, the next *musts* are unavoidably clear.

>If we want spiritual power, we MUST know the Word of God.

>If we want our children to have spiritual power, We MUST teach our children the Word of God.

This, then, is the cornerstone--the foundation of a program of discipline that cannot fail:

We Must Teach Our Children The Word Of God.

Chapter Five

Teaching "The Four Rs": What MUST A Child Know?

The First R

Can you figure out what the statements have in common?

"It doesn't really matter what you believe, as long as you're sincere.

"We all worship the same God anyway, so what's the problem if we don't agree on the details?"

"We're all going to the same place. We just happen to have different ways of getting there, that's all."

"I live a good life. I try not to hurt anybody, and to be accepting of others. What more could God want?"

"You don't really believe that a loving God would be so cruel that He would condemn somebody for not believing in Christ!"

And, of course, there's the old standby:

"What about the natives in Africa . . .?"

There's no question that you've probably heard most, if not all, of these statements, in one variation or another. What they all have in common is that they attack the central teaching of Jesus Christ. Jesus says that only through faith in Him can we attain personal righteousness before God.

It's not possible to avoid hearing the "many ways to God" philosophy embodied in these statements. In one way or another, it is repeated in social gatherings, on television, in the public schools, at work, and especially on college campuses. For example, one of the most admired women in America, whose opinions influence millions of people, expressed the philosophy this way:

"One of the biggest mistakes humans make is to believe that there is only one way. Actually, there are many diverse paths leading to what you call God."

What's The Big Deal About *That*?

Here's what's so dangerous about the statements above, including Oprah's statement. Not one of these statements is a direct, hostile, readily observable challenge

54

to your child's salvation. *And that is precisely why each statement is a deadly threat to your child's faith!*

If someone were to come up to your child and say:

> "There is no God."
> "Christ is not God's Son."
> "Jesus did not rise from the dead."
> "There will be no resurrection of the dead,"

or some similarly blatant challenge to the basic tenets of Christianity, your child would be immediately on guard. There is something about a direct, frontal assault on our faith that often brings out the best in us. But the problem with the first set of statements is that there is no observable, direct assault. Like Satan, the statements are subtle.

The Trap

What is offered is compromise, under the guise of *accommodation.* And that is a trap. Stated in a different way, what is being said is this: "You accept my ideas, and I'll accept yours." This implies that your idea about what's right is just as correct as my idea about what's right. And then our ideas about what's right are no different than so and so's ideas about what's right. Because, as the words of one popular song declare, "We're all God's children." If this is so, then there really isn't any need to preach the gospel of salvation through Jesus Christ, because there really isn't any need for Christ. So it really doesn't make any difference whether Jesus is God's Son or not. Or whether He rose from the dead. Now, see what happens. The end result of a friendly "accommodation" is really worse than the end result of a direct frontal assault on your child's faith.   Your child's beliefs have been compromised. Because not only is your child's faith contaminated, corrupted, perverted, and destroyed; he doesn't even know what hit him!

Nobody ever argues against ideas like "acceptance" and "tolerance" and "understanding," and other similar-sounding themes. These are all desirable behaviors which should be followed by the Christian, but not at the expense of watering down or sacrificing the essence of his own faith. There is a monumental difference between "accommodation" and "acceptance." And there's a world of difference between "accommodating" somebody else's ideas to honor the person's Constitutional rights, and "compromising" with somebody by giving in on some value that's really important to you, just to get along with others.

A Jew Who Has No Respect for Christians--For a Reason That Will Surprise You!

Let me give you an example of the difference between "accommodation" and "compromise." One of my closest friends from the university faculty is a devout Jew, who is a sincere follower of Judaism. We enjoy one another's company, and we care for each other a great deal. Yet I make no bones about the fact that I am distraught because my Jewish friend, Norman, does not accept Jesus Christ as the Messiah. Norman is well aware I believe that faith in Jesus Christ is essential for salvation. When Norman honored me and my family by inviting us to his home to celebrate Passover Seder with his family, we were pleased to be held in such high esteem. But I told Norman, "If the Passover Seder includes a prayer that the Messiah will come to the Jews, you know that we can't celebrate Seder with you, because you know that we believe that the Messiah has already come for your family and for my family in the person of Jesus Christ."

Norman knows that I love him. Norman accepts me as his friend. I accept Norman as my friend. Norman accepts the fact that I believe that faith in Jesus Christ is necessary for salvation. He accepts the fact *that* I believe, but he does not accept *what* I believe. I accept the fact that Norman *believes* that his approach to God is valid. In our relationship, then, Norman and I accept our differences and we respect one another's right to believe as each wishes, but we do not tell one another that, after all, "It really doesn't make any difference what you believe. It's the same God, isn't it?" Neither of us *accommodates* himself or his beliefs to what we believe is not true. We accommodate the other person insofar as we do not try to stifle one another. But we do not *compromise* our beliefs just to get along. In fact, Norman, who is currently a talk radio host, has even asked me, on the air, to explicitly repeat for his audience what I have often told him in private: That Jesus said, *"I am the Way, the Truth, and the Life. No man comes to the father but by Me."* He has also asked me to cite the verse, *"He Who has the Son, has Life. He Who has not the Son, does not have Life."* He

57

does this to illustrate to his listeners that he has respect for a Christian who will not water down what the Bible says, just to "be nice" to a Jew.

Norman declares that he has absolutely no use for Christians who mutter some mealy-mouthed half-explanation about "God's special relationship with the Jews," just so that they can avoid offending him by telling him that he needs Jesus. Norman actually *baits* Christians to see whether they will stand up for their beliefs, or whether they will collapse like a house of cards at the first wind of discomfort. And when they soft-pedal their faith, he publicly rebukes them for their failure to stand up for Jesus! Their fear of offending him, in fact, is what offends him most! You see, Norman and I both understand that there is no room for compromise on life and death issues, and we do not water down our beliefs so that others will accept us, or so that we will not make the other person uncomfortable.

But we are adults. American kids, on the other hand, want so desperately to be accepted, and are so thoroughly indoctrinated in school with the idea that cooperation and "consensus building" are to be valued above all things, that they will not be able to avoid caving in to teacher and peer pressure. In fact, one of the criticisms of Outcome-Based Education and the U.S. Department of Education's Goals 2000 was the very fact that teachers who wanted to foist their values off on their pupils had the power to give children a grade based on whether students would "cooperate" in "achieving consensus"--otherwise known as "group agreement." Christian kids, whose values were different from those of the world, didn't have a chance! Truly, they were in a situation of "To get along, you must go along."

What I have been saying so far, obviously, is that it really *does* matter what you believe. In fact, it's a matter of life and death.

The First R: The Truth About Righteousness

That makes it easy to identify the first **must** that we teach our child about the Scriptures. It's the first of *"The Four Rs"*. The truth about *Righteousness*.

First, we MUST teach our child that the Scriptures declare in brilliantly lucid testimony, that faith in Jesus Christ is necessary for salvation. That this truth is the cornerstone--the Rock--upon which we build our hope. That *nothing else* but faith in Christ will ever satisfy God.

Second, we MUST teach our child, by memory, the specific verses which testify to this fact.

If we do these two **musts**, we can be unwaveringly confident of two things:

(1) Our child will be able to withstand not only a direct frontal assault on his faith. Our child will recognize the dangers of accommodation. He will not be a victim of what *sounds* good. In short, *he will be so well-grounded in the truth that he will not be deceived.*

(2) What is equally important, he will be so firmly committed that *he will not cave in* under peer pressure, teacher disapproval, or intellectual gymnastics.

59

How Your Child Will be Slam-Dunked:

The very first attack on your child's faith will be an attack on the core belief of Christianity: That salvation and eternal life come through Jesus Christ. Your child will be bombarded with powerful arguments from every quarter, and the arguments will be relentless, persuasive, and encountered everywhere.

I wish I could show you the term paper a Christian student left in my mailbox at the university. He had been assigned to write a "Reflective Paper"--one of his first term papers at the university. His professor had told the students to write their reactions to what they had learned in the course to that point. Assuming that the professor genuinely wanted to find out what students were thinking, the young man diligently completed his assignment, in which he transcribed his thoughts on the content of the first part of a course on *Pluralism and Multiculturalism,* a course which is often laced with heavy "politically correct" content and pro-homosexual propaganda.

To introduce his paper, the student quoted a Christian newsletter his parents received on a regular basis, and compared what he had heard in class with the values he had been taught at home, and which were articulately stated in the newsletter. Without going into detail on what the student wrote, I can summarize like this: What the student said--accurately, I might add-- was that, although all kinds of points-of-view, including homosexuality, atheism, and "alternative life styles" were not only tolerated, but actually promoted, in the public schools, the only perspective that was excluded was Christianity. He also asserted--again, correctly--the fact that the Great Documents of the United States had, as their foundation, the Holy Scriptures. And he remarked that it was hard to understand, therefore, why Scriptural points of view were systematically derided, or totally excluded, from classroom discussions of morality and ethics.

Here are some of the professor's handwritten comments, scrawled in screaming letters across the margins of the student's paper:

>In response to the student's thoughts on atheism and moral relativism, the professor scribbled, *"Who is to say that Christianity is the only way to Spirituality?!"* (Can you see, here, the first assault on the Christian belief about how we attain right standing with God through the blood of Jesus Christ?)

>Reacting to the student's assertion that Christians are persecuted by the adherents of atheism, socialism, and witchcraft, the professor scrawled, half in cursive and half in printed block letters, almost to the point where one could read her emotionalism between the lines: *"Again-- Christians stir up anger and confusion, based on faulty information. They desire* STATUS QUO!"

>Editorializing on the student's observation that Christian values have been virtually totally excluded from discussions of ethics and morality, the professor again spewed out her biases, writing across the margin:

"WRONG--*They are ingrained in every part of the system!*

This student's experience, by the way, is not unusual. The only unusual aspect of this particular example is that I didn't even know the student who left the paper in my campus mailbox! He had been so intellectually and emotionally beaten up by an anti-Christian professor, that he was driven to seek help from a faculty member he had never met! Traditionalist Christian kids--those who believe what God says, and who cling to Jesus as the only way to salvation--are being intellectually assaulted and spiritually molested on the university campus and in the majority of public school classrooms. *And most parents are not preparing them for the assault!*

The Apostle Paul exhorted us to be aware of the danger of compromise, and described how human beings would substitute their own ideas of right and wrong for the truth. He warned about the problem of the persuasive appeal of scintillating rhetoric and brilliantly-devised and cleverly-crafted arguments. He alerted us to what we would face: *"See to it,"* he declared, *"that no one makes a prey of you by philosophy and empty deceit, according to human tradition . . . "* (Colossians 2:8 KJV).

Another Inescapable Conclusion:

We absolutely MUST teach"The First R". When we do so, the second thing about which we can be confident is this:

Our child will be able to cite the only final authority on the subject, the Scripture itself, in support of his faith. He will not be left to depend upon immature or not-fully-developed powers of argumentation, rhetoric, or logic. He will not need to. He will be guarded by the mighty power of the Word of God. *Because we have taught him* what he MUST know, he will be able to say, with the Apostle Paul:

I use God's mighty weapons, not those made by men, to knock down the devil's strongholds. These weapons can break down every proud argument against God and every wall that can be built to keep men from finding Him. With these weapons I can capture rebels and bring them back to God, and change them into men whose hearts' desire is obedience to Christ. (2 Corinthians 10:4,5) (TLB)

Now, I'm not advocating, here, that we urge our children to enter the arena of verbal and philosophical combat with teachers or professors who have made a career of attacking traditional values. Not at all. The Scriptures we teach our children will be, first and foremost, a defense against attacks. The Holy Spirit will, as Jesus promised, remind them of everything God has taught them.

In time, our children will be called upon to heed Paul's admonition to *"always be ready to defend the hope you have, but be gentle and respectful."* But they will always be protected by the discernment they've gained through God's Word, so that they will know when to speak, and when to refrain from *"casting pearls before swine."* or *"giving that which is holy unto the dogs."*

They will not be torn to pieces.

They will be strong in the Lord.

Chapter Six

Teaching the Second R:
Resistance

The 11th Commandment: "Thou shalt say it's okay if . . ."

One of the courses I teach at the university has a whole section on how to teach children critical reading and critical thinking. One of the problems of teaching these skills is that the ways in which we are influenced are so subtle that we often don't even know we've been "had" until somebody explicitly points it out. An example I always use is to ask this question: "Do you remember Nushawn Williams?" Invariably, I am met with silence.

"I'll give you a few hints," I continue. "He lived in upstate New York--Chautauqua County, to be exact. There were over a dozen women and young girls, including a fifteen- year- old. He went to jail . . .."

At this point, several hands usually shoot into the air, and participants correctly identify Nushawn Williams as a man who committed a gross moral offense: He was HIV positive, and he victimized a host of women by having unprotected sex with them! My audiences-- especially my college students -- are shocked at the immorality of the man; imagine--having unprotected sex when you know you're HIV positive--and not telling your partners!

What never ceases to amaze me is that no-one ever condemns Nushawn Williams for being an unrestrained, licentious fornicator. No one ever says he's immoral because of his sexual promiscuity. No. Not at all. That's not even a consideration. Nushawn Williams is immoral because he broke the first and greatest commandment on the college campus. He did the unthinkable. He committed the unforgivable: He practiced Unsafe Sex!

The New Logic of Sexual Morality:

Let me show you where this insane thinking came from. Suppose I were to say to you, "We're going backpacking in the Colorado mountains, but there is a forecast of a storm front moving in. Would it be good, or bad, to take extra precautions to be sure that we have a safe hike?" Naturally, you'd respond that it would be good to be safe, and, conversely, it would be a bad decision to be unsafe. Suppose I then followed with this question: "You're going to be driving on Interstate 29 through North Dakota in January. Someone suggests that you take some extra blankets, a cell phone, emergency foodstuffs, and a catalytic heater, and maybe some tire chains. Would that advice be good, or bad?" Naturally, you'd respond that the advice would be good. To take precautions to be safe would be good. To ignore the advice would be bad--

reckless, even. And if your foolhardiness endangered others, it would not only be unsafe. It would be *immoral*.

Now let's get to the "logic", which is accepted, without question, in high schools and on university campuses across the country. It's sort of like a mathematical equation. It's a false logic that leads people to condemn Nushawn Williams, but not for the right reason.

The equation goes like this in the minds of many people--and not only young people:

"If it is good to be safe, and if it is bad to be unsafe, then it logically follows that:

Safe = Good.

and

Unsafe= Bad.

It therefore follows that

Safe *Sex*= Good,

and

Unsafe *Sex*= Bad.

"Therefore, if I am responsible, I will practice Safe Sex. I will have done good. I will have made a moral decision.

I will deserve to be praised.
Safe is Good.
My actions are Good.
I am Good. "

You can see, then, how easy it is for even Christians to fall prey to the prevailing sexual ethos. Because, invariably, according to my university students, the immorality of Nushawn Williams is not that he lasciviously indulged himself in wanton sexual promiscuity--it's that he didn't practice Safe Sex! In other words, not only does society *not* condemn fornication as "wrong". It praises those who fornicate "safely", "respectfully", and "responsibly!" And make no mistake about it. Even Christian young people are vulnerable to this line of argument, because it comes at them from so many otherwise respectable quarters that they are spiritually, emotionally, and intellectually beaten to a pulp, without even knowing what happened.

How Are Kids Prepared by the Enemy for Moral Insanity?

The insidious rotting away of our moral moorings didn't happen overnight. If you're a parent of young children, you probably remember these words from a highly popular song:

"I took you to an intimate restaurant, Then to a suggestive movie. There's nothing left to talk about 'less it's horizontally. Let's get physical..... I wanna' get physical. . . Let's get animal..... I wanna' get animal. . ."

These words, from the hit song "*Physical*" by Olivia Newton-John, which hit the top of the charts to usher in the year 1982, were a part of an insidiously seductive philosophy celebrated by other popular entertainers. The Pointer Sisters purred in their hit song, *Slow Hand*, about the lover who would "say it's all right" if they "want it all night," and who would not "come and go in a heated rush." And at the same time that our kids were learning techniques on how to get "physical" they were learning some new lessons about the devil. To be sure, he wasn't the horrible satanic power the Bible describes. In fact, there he was, "in blue eyes and blue jeans"--as described by Terry Gibbs in his song "*Somebody's Knockin*", and it was hard not to let him in. Indeed, other celebrities encouraged kids to ignore their parents, as the lyrics of a popular song by Rod Stewart so clearly illustrated in 1982:

> *Young hearts, be free tonight*
> *Time is one your side ...*
> *Don't let 'em put you down*
> *Don't let 'em push you 'round,*
> *Don't ever let them change your*
> *point of view ...(Young Turks)*

Obviously, the "them" in Rod Stewart's song didn't refer to kids' friends, and if we had any doubt about it, the song continues to tell us how Billy and Patty "just ran away" because "there's no point in talkin' when nobody's lis'nen', " meaning, presumably, that if parents were really "lis'nen' "they'd accede to their teenagers' torrid and uncontrollable desire to "get physical."

68

Adults, too, were encouraged by pop and country western music in the eighties to violate scriptural standards of morality. Alice, in the song, "Alice Doesn't Live Here Anymore," simply tacks a note on the door and wanders off in pursuit of personal "fulfillment," leaving behind her husband and two children, who, when they have recovered from the initial shock of having their wife and mother disappear without warning, will presumably follow her instructions to tell their friends and neighbors what the note says; namely, that Alice's desertion is to be excused, because "Alice doesn't live here anymore."

Why Are We Surprised?

The changes we see in morals and values today didn't happen overnight, or dramatically. They were extremely subtle. It shouldn't be a surprise to us when a man or a woman walks out of a marriage to have a sexual tryst with some stranger they met on an Internet "Chat Room." The stage was set for moral anarchy years ago! We were just sleeping, that's all!

Some readers might remember when Bruce Springsteen, in his song, *"Hungry Heart,"* banged out with cavalier abandon the excuse that he left his wife and children behind after deciding that his wrong turn on the freeway might lead to greater "fulfillment" than returning home. His excuse was, as we all know, "everybody's got a hungry heart."

Even the music of a woman whose Christian witness in the late '90s bore powerful testimony to Jesus Christ in such hostile environments as a Las Vegas casino stage dulled the consciences of her Christian fans. The

69

beautiful and popular Barbara Mandrell's *If Lovin' You is Wrong, I Don't Wanna' be Right,* was appealingly heart-tugging--mild, actually, compared to tons of songs that justified adulterous affairs. And whether the words of the songs were consciously considered or merely unconsciously hummed and repeated, they were creating a different perspective about moral behavior. The onslaught of sexual escapades of sports heroes, entertainers, media personalities, evangelists, and even the President of the United States was soon to follow. We failed to "guard the truth" God entrusted us with, and the result was a climate of sensuality that would have assigned Sodom and Gomorra a "PG" rating if it were a contemporary movie.

What Are We Missing?

While popular songs, starting in the eighties and dancing through the nineties, were spewing out acceptance and advocacy of new standards of abominable behavior which went right over the heads of most parents and right into the heads of most of their children, many concerned parents in the eighties were missing the real danger. They strained their ears to discover whether it was really true that if you were to play some records backwards, you would hear flagrant, blatant, unconcealed denunciation of all that is holy. And while they clucked their disapproval of what they heard when certain records were played backwards, their children, who could easily fend off the gimmick as an obvious attempt of record promoters to stimulate sales, were being seduced by the widespread acceptance of the philosophies advocated by lyrics their parents did not seem to hear.

Where's the Problem?

Most parents these days are no different. We rail against rap and MTV and boycott the panderers of perversion only when it's so blatant it would cause blushing in a bordello. But we missed what we should have seen, because, like it or not, we've been desensitized by contemporary culture. Forget about the Internet, and the assault on morality that's available at the click of a mouse. There are other deadly dangers to our kids that we don't even see.

Many of us missed the deadly message of the "love scene" in *Titanic* and other films like it. The fornication between the two young people who had barely time to remember one another's names was glorified as "redeeming." The notion that a young woman would disrobe and pose naked for a near-stranger was accepted as "just natural."

What could parents have been thinking--especially Christian parents, in allowing their children to see Titanic? Indeed, in one fifth-grade Sunday school class of close to a score of children, only one child had not been accosted by Hollywood's assault on historical truth-- blatant sex notwithstanding. The rest, some of whom had seen it more than once--were undoubtedly the offspring of well-meaning parents who gushed with delight that Precious was, at long last, interested in real history!

Many Christian parents are also clueless about the alluring lyrics, provocative clothing and contaminating choreography of

7 1

seemingly innocent country western videos. Just like the blind guides rebuked by Jesus; we parents "strain at a gnat, and swallow a camel." We seem to worry about hairstyles, jewelry, clothing, and makeup. We have more concern about what is put *on* our kids' heads than what is going *into* our kids' heads.

Here's what we need to think about: What is so dangerous about the lyrics and videos of country western or popular music? Or the subtle values transmitted by "classic" movies? *What is so dangerous is the fact that hardly anybody regards them as dangerous.* That's right. What is dangerous is that hardly anybody regards them as dangerous. The reason? Well, how can they be dangerous if they represent what is a common set of values in the Western world today? The behaviors and customs--the social mores nowadays (remember that word "nowadays"?) are directed toward self-actualization, or personal fulfillment. Everybody's looking for fulfillment, much like Sarah in the preceding chapter. As a result, we have a lot of "practical" and "realistic" ideas which are taken for granted in today's society. Examples? Prenuptial agreements before a marriage ceremony, to take care of any problems a divorce might bring just in case the marriage doesn't work out. We have Christian parents who tolerate their offspring co-habitating (read "shacking up") with their "significant other", and who whine an acquiescent, "Well, what can you do?" in reflecting upon the debauchery of their children.

The famous and the not-so-famous, including our co-workers and our neighbors, tell us that we have a "right" to be "happy." Commitment just doesn't count any more. As the words of many

72

popular songs indicate, that right includes the right to "split" if you don't "get off" on your marriage. Commitment is still a part of our society. Only this time around it's commitment to personal happiness, not commitment to Jesus Christ, or commitment to others. Sleeping around is okay, suggest the lyrics of popular songs, as long as you don't hurt anybody, which supposedly means that you can have sex with anybody—male or female or both at the same time--as long as there is willingness on the part of all participants. And, of course, as long as you're discreet, and you obey "the first and Greatest Commandment: Thou shalt practice Safe Sex. "

"The Second Great Commandment: Your Attitude is What's Important"

Make no mistake about it. There is a new philosophy afoot which has infected an astounding number of Christian young people. Here's the philosophy, in a nutshell, that passes for virtue on college campuses. You are a "good person" if you follow it. It actually started long ago--around 1929, when Bertrand Russell, in *Marriage and Morals*, wrote these words:

"Morality in sexual relations, when it is free from superstition, consists essentially of respect for the other person, and unwillingness to use that person solely as a means of personal gratification, without regard to his or her desires."

By the way, the "superstition" that Bertrand Russell was talking about is stuff like the Ten Commandments, which media mogul Ted Turner, in the late '90s, declared to be outdated, no longer applicable, and, to be sure, the cause of many problems in modern society! In fact, according to Turner, the prohibition against adultery ought to be totally abolished; "Nowadays," (there's that word again!) opines Turner, "it just doesn't work."

Even Christians Cave In

I cannot even count how many times I've had students in my classes who, once they discovered that I was a Christian, communicated to me in one way or another that they, too, were Christian. That was always an encouragement to me, but, sad to say, in about fifty per cent of the cases, I was soon to be disappointed. I would discover--sometimes in a casual conversation, sometimes via a telephone call to let them know about a test or some other detail, that they were living with their boyfriend or girlfriend. They had no qualms at all about being sexually intimate, because, after all, their love was genuine and true, they intended to get engaged or married when they graduated, and they were not just "sleeping around" for sexual gratification. I am no longer surprised when Christian adults who are single or divorced freely engage in sexual activity because they have substituted the philosophy of the Bertrand Russells, the Dr. Ruths, and other sirens of the sexual revolution, for the clear and earnest exhortations of the Scriptures. There is a set of values in the Western world that pervades our music, our

74

recreation, our sports, our entertainment, our tastes in clothing--in sum, our whole society. Our children are assailed by stimuli which can blind them and deafen them to the way of Jesus Christ.

Now, if all this were a direct frontal assault, I wouldn't be as deeply concerned as I am. A direct frontal assault can be defended against. I could say, "You're going to be assaulted and blinded by a searchlight. Watch for it! Cover your eyes immediately, and you won't be blinded!" But the destructive values of our society don't blind our kids like the sudden and brilliant glare of a searchlight. They are much more insidious and treacherous. They move in like a cold, damp, fog which silently steals inland, engulfing and surrounding everything. No one is aware of just when the fog moved in. No one knows where the fog came from. It is just suddenly there. Without warning. And it blinds one to danger just as surely and completely as the blinding assault of a powerful, high-intensity searchlight. We find ourselves, if we are ever fortunate enough to pause and reflect on what is going on around us, accepting and tolerating things because "times have changed." Nowadays. . . .

But what does God have to say about how we are to react? God Almighty, in His Word, says,

Don't copy the behavior and customs of this world, but be a new and different person, with a fresh newness in all you do and think. Then you will learn, from your own experience, how His ways will really satisfy you. (Romans 12:2 TLB)

The King James Bible puts it this way: *"Be ye not conformed to this world, but be ye transformed, by the renewing of your minds. .. "*

That Discomfort You Feel is a Good Sign

Scripture tells us that we are strangers and foreigners in a strange land. When we are in a foreign country, with strange customs, different values, and ways of doing things that are not the way we do them, we should feel discomfort. Unfortunately, though, on the university campus and in many public schools, Christian kids are made to feel that they and their bigotted Christian families are the cause of most of the discomfort in society, and if only they would quit judging everybody else, everyone would be a lot happier.

Our children --and we--need to remember this:

What God says, and what society--the world--says are *diametric opposites!* They are two totally different ways of

> thinking
> believing
> acting
> behaving
> living.

There is *no possibility* of walking with the Word and of walking with the world at the same time. There is *no way* that we can serve God, and also serve ourselves. If we try it, the Bible is quite direct about what the result will be. Jesus Himself said:

"You cannot serve two masters. . ." *(Matthew 6:24)*.

If we are really serving the Master, then we have to be completely different from the world. *"You are living a brand new kind of life,"* Paul tells us in *Colossians 3: 10,11, "where whether a person has Christ is what matters. . . . "*

The Choice is Clear:

"If you be unwilling to serve the Lord, choose this day whom you will serve, " we are directed in Joshua 24:15. But, knowing what we know, we have made our choice. And the choice is undeniably clear. The next must, then, is also unavoidably clear:

Besides teaching our children to memorize Scripture which will enable them to argue against the debilitating arguments of universalism or other attractive religious philosophies which deny that Jesus Christ is the Savior, we *must* teach our children to memorize Scripture which will enable *them to Resist the destructive values of contemporary society.*

What Your Child Should be Able to Do:

We can prepare our children for any circumstance they are likely to run into.

Let me give you just a few examples of what I mean when I say that children **must** know by memory Scriptures which will enable them to resist the seductive allure of the values of today's world:

(1) A popular argument that pervades our culture, and which became painfully obvious during the scandal of the Clinton administration, was the "Do your own thing" philosophy. This philosophy says, "You do what you want, I do what I want; we don't get on each other's case": A sample argument about what God says is found in Matthew 5:13-16. There, followers of Jesus are told that we have the responsibility to make any group "different" just because we are in it--and that if it isn't noticeably different because we're there, there's something wrong with us.

(2) Another philosophy our kids are hit with is the "When in Rome, do as the Romans do" philosophy. Namely, that if they don't like something, they ought to get off everybody else's case, or "get out." Colossians 3:17 blows this philosophy right out of the water, telling us that we are representatives of the Lord Jesus in whatever we do or say.

(3)   Here's a sample argument against the idea that says that we have a "right" to be happy and to go after those things which will make us happy. (The old *materialism* argument, so persuasively asserted by none other than Madonna, in her popular hit song, "*Material Girl*", which was blithely parroted by literally thousands of Christian kids): Philippians 1:21 is dynamite, but most Christians can't handle it. Nevertheless, children who are trained up in the way they should go will be able, as adults, to live the verse: "For to me, living means opportunities for Christ," or, as the King James version so succinctly translates it: "To live, is Christ."

And then, of course, there's the "I can't help it" whimpering which is used repeatedly as a part of the "it's only natural" school of excuses: (This argument is a favorite of the homosexual lobby, which repeatedly uses the words, "sexual *orientation*", otherwise known as the "I was born this way" argument, instead of "sexual *preference*," *or* the "I choose to live this way" argument). The Scriptures tell us that what is natural is *not* acceptable (Romans 8:7,8) and that God will help us to do what is not natural for us (Philippians 4:13).

(5)   Sample argument against a "Me first" philosophy:
"*Don't just be interested in your own affairs, but be interested in others, too, and what they are doing*" (*Philippians 2:4 TLB*).

79

The Arguments are Age-Old--But so is the Defense!

A thick reference book could be written, classifying all the popular and socially acceptable arguments supporting almost any behavior short of vicious homicide or violent sexual assault. The important fact to remember, though, is that *only the power of the Scripture can stand up against the relentless onslaught of the values of the world.*

Some of the most crafty, clever, and deviously brilliant minds at the time of Jesus plotted intricately conceived intellectual snares for Jesus in an attempt to publicly humiliate Him and diminish the impact of His teaching. But Jesus had personal intellectual and expressive powers that were so unlimited that He demolished the arguments of His critics with a display of reasoning which, we are told, so overwhelmed them that they *"dared not ask Him any more questions."*

There's one other vitally significant fact which we should not miss: Despite the fact that Jesus could slice through logical arguments and cut them to pieces like an expert fencer wielding a finely-honed rapier, he did not resort to the power of his intellectual capacity. *In every instance in which He was confronted with the appeal of the values of the world, the Son of God responded by quoting Scripture!* There can be no more powerful reason for arming our children with the Word of God to enable them to stand firm and steadfast as they are assailed with the seemingly sweet reasonableness of worldly values.

So we now have two **musts**, both of which deal with the memorization of the Scripture:

(1)   We MUST teach our children verses which prove that Jesus Christ is the *only* way to eternal life.

(2)   We MUST teach our children verses which will enable them to confront and resist the temptations of contemporary values.

Chapter Seven

Freaking Out is Not an Option: Teaching the Third R: Recovery

There is also a third **must** in memorizing Scripture which leads to discipline that can't fail. Think about this for a minute. How is our faith challenged? We have listed only two ways so far:

(1) Compromising with beliefs which deny Jesus as the Savior. (Confusion about *Righteousness*).

(2) Attraction to spiritually destructive values of the world. (A Lack of *Resistance*).

Crazy Ideas About God's Grace:

You've probably wondered about some of the crazy ideas some Christians get when they experience trouble. One Christian father, whose son's promising high school athletic career was cut short by an automobile accident told me, "God hurt my son because He is punishing me for something." As though Christ's death were not sufficient payment for their sins, and as though God would kill other people or make other people suffer to punish big, egocentric ME! Think about it! Many Christians suffer great anxiety for their loved ones--even after accepting Christ's forgiveness and committing their loved ones to God's care, because they believe that they, the parents, are so important that God would maim, cripple, or kill a loved one to "punish" a transgressing parent! And they are fed even more foolishness by well-meaning Christian friends, who, like the friends of Job in the Old Testament, tell them that if they are "right" with God, health and wealth would be sure to follow. (Obviously, they've either never read, or have forgotten entirely, Paul's narrative of all of his troubles, including shipwreck, prison, beatings, and other tribulations he suffered because he was obedient to God in spreading the Gospel!)

Because these Christians do not know the Scriptures-because they do not "meditate on them day and night"--because they do not "bind them about their hearts," they are misled by the father of lies, Satan, into bitterness, weakened prayer life, complaining, wavering and vascillating faith, or destructive beliefs. Suppose that the Apostle Peter, suffering in prison, would have whimpered, "God is punishing me. I knew he'd get me for denying Jesus."

The Challenge of Life's Troubles:

The third way our faith is challenged is through *trouble, or adversity.* I have counseled *many* college students who have told me, "If there *was* a God, He wouldn't let this happen to me." Even Christian adults who have suddenly had their idyllic lives shaken by trouble have stopped praying, they have complained bitterly, and they have had their faith seriously damaged. The Scripture tells us that the children of Israel "murmured" against the Lord when things didn't seem to be going well. People really haven't changed much in the last several thousand years, and they still murmur against God when things aren't going their way.

The Plane Crash: Faith Tested to the Limit

Let's go back, for a second, to the example of the anxious, uncertain speculation of ill-informed Christians who think God is "getting them" for something they did wrong. Compare their attitude with the testimony of Steve Smart, of Port Mansfield, Texas. He survived a faith-challenging ordeal in the life-threatening high country of the Colorado mountains. His story, and the story of his companions, was carried on the front page in successive issues of the *Denver Post* on December 30 and December 31 of 1981, beginning with the headline on December 30, *"'Miracle' Rescue Saves Four Texans Five Days After Mountain Crash."* Excerpts from the story read:

Deciding to make one last attempt after five days of searching, rescuers following a weak radio signal trudged through 7-foot-deep snow Tuesday afternoon and discovered four injured persons huddled in the wreckage of a small plane at the 11,600-foot level of Mount Columbia.

One pilot-doctor told The Denver Post it was a "miracle" that the victims survived hurricane-force winds earlier this week which caused a wind-chill factor reaching 60 degrees below zero in the Colorado Rockies 100 air miles southwest of Denver. A fifth victim--the pilot--had walked from the plane after it crashed on Christmas Eve to seek help. There was no trace of him, the rescue party reported . . .

In the story the next day, the real drama was revealed by another survivor, Patricia Meeks:

"After we landed (On the afternoon of Christmas Eve) the weather really got bad, snowing and blowing snow. Sometimes we couldn't even see the tops of the trees," Mrs. Meeks said, adding that at other times they could see circling planes and helicopters but probably couldn't be seen because of the snow covering their plane at the edge of the tree line.

85

"When the rescuers arrived. . . Mrs. Meeks was reading the Bible," Smart said, "at the passage as to why God lets us suffer. . . . We never gave up hope," Smart said. . . "Never. We just made our peace up there, and if somebody wants to rescue us, we'd consent to serving Jesus here, and if they didn't, we'd just join Him."

There was another miracle connected to the dramatic rescue: Steve Smart's picture, accompanied by his dynamic testimony in large, boldface type, was featured, along with the rest of the story, on the front page of *The Denver Post!*

Was It Just an Emotional High?

But were the stirring words of Steve Smart merely an expected, uncontrollable emotional outpouring of relief upon being rescued? Was he having a kind of temporary "spiritual high" which is often encountered in crisis, but which just as often vanishes as soon as the immediate crisis is over? Or was his testimony genuine evidence that there are, indeed, Christians like Steve Smart who lean on the Word of God and who are able to share their faith with others in the time of their most challenging ordeal?

A *Temporary* High Doesn't Last a Year!

Almost exactly one year later, on December 26, 1982, Steve Smart, this time literally on his knees--for his legs had been amputated below the knee because of frostbite complications--was again pictured and quoted in the *Denver Post*. The *Post* ran an anniversary story of the miracle rescue, and again Steve Smart provided an unwavering reaffirmation of his relationship with a personal God. And once again, the story was front page news. This time, it was Patricia Meeks' picture and accompanying testimony, in boldface type, which graced the story, highlighting a headline which read, *"Faith, Hope 2 Legacies of Rockies Plane Crash"*: "There is something else here that God wants us to do. There has to be some reason why we didn't all die up there," Mrs. Meeks asserted.

Even a year later, the faith of two Christians, one of whom lost his legs, and the other who lost her husband, remained bold and unwavering. In fact, it was even stronger in the face of adversity!

Other Resistance Under Adversity:

Two other committed Christians, Jeff and Suzie Wilkinson, whose personal ordeal and courageous testimony of faith, like Steve Smart's and Patricia Meeks' story and testimony, was also bannered in a front-page *Denver Post* feature story, provided additional evidence of the strength dedicated Christians find in the word of God. The Wilkinson's youngest child, two-year-old Hannah, remained in a coma six weeks after she was sucked into a rain-choked underground irrigation pipe on the Wilkinson ranch, south of Grand Junction, Colorado, on the Western Slope of the Rockies. *Denver Post* staff writer Tom Coakley interviewed Jeff Wilkinson, reporting that, "for strength, the couple has turned often to the Bible and what God says about trusting in Him and about the value of tribulation in life."

"We're holding up all right," Coakley quoted Jeff Wilkinson as saying. "You see, the thing about this is that the Lord loves her more than I do. At first that was a hard pill for me to choke, but He does. The Lord lends us a child just like he lends you your life."

Jeff's wife, Suzie, provided an equally moving and eloquent testimony to her conviction that a loving God was in charge of the lives of her children. Said Suzie Wilkinson of the hours immediately following Hannah's accident, ". . . I had this inner peace, knowing if she wasn't going to be with me, she would be with the Lord; but the first night was the worst." (*Denver Post,* October 10, 1982).

It Can't Get Any Worse Than This: The Last Will and Testament of Shari Smith

"Last Will and Testament." This was what was written at the top of the last words Bob and Hilda Smith ever heard from their seventeen-year-old daughter, Shari. Only twelve hours earlier, in the middle of the afternoon

of May 31, 1985, Bob had found Shari's car in the driveway with the engine running and the door open. Shari's purse was on the seat. Shari was nowhere in sight.

A series of sadistic telephone calls from a psychopathic kidnapper compounded the agony of the Smith family. Six days later, following a massive search, Shari's body was found. She had been brutally raped and murdered.

While none of us will ever know, in this life, how the Smith family must have suffered, the words of Shari's Last Will and Testament ease some of the anguish that we feel for Shari and her family. She was at the mercy of a brutal killer. She was almost certainly aware that she would be murdered. And yet, in the depths of the darkest caverns of the night, Shari wrote these words to her family:

"I'll be with my Father now, so please don't worry! Don't ever let this ruin your lives, and keep living one day at a time for Jesus. My thoughts will always be with you. Everything works out for the good of those that love God."

Could any Christian possibly miss the brilliantly clear fact that Shari Smith was strengthened by the power of the Holy Spirit, working through the Word of God? Shari Smith--helpless, suffering at the hands of her abductor, and knowing what lay ahead, was able to comfort her survivors! Her words testify to the fact that she was able to endure because "the peace of God which passes all understanding"(Philippians 4:7) was hers. It sustained her in her final hours. And God's peace was present in such abundance that her final words were the words of Romans 8:28.

My files are full of accounts of children and young people who were able to endure adversity, face death, and overcome personal failures because they were lifted up by the power of the Word of God.

I know that the point I am trying to make about the cruciality of the word of God for Recovery has been made. Nevertheless, I cannot leave these pages without sharing two more stories--each of which has a lesson in it for us.

Other Last Words of Power in the Face of Adversity:

Quite different from Shari Smith's trauma, but the same in the power of the last words of a child to his parents, is the inspiring account of what happened in the lives of Ron and LaVonne Masters. Their book, *"Some Through the Flood,"* is a stirring recounting of their ordeal during a horrible flash flood in the Black Hills of South Dakota. Among those who lost their lives in the catastrophe were the Masters' three sons. In mere seconds, a raging torrent picked up the family car like a piece of cork, and the swirling waters surged through the car windows and engulfed the family.

Masters recalled, " . . .in a matter of seconds, the water was up to our necks . . . My oldest boy, Steve, said, 'Dad, this is all in God's hands.' Those were the last words we ever heard from Steve."

About their book, which chronicles their night of terror clinging, in the pitch black of night, to a cottonwood tree. and the ultimate survival of their two daughters, La Vonne Masters had this to say: "The thesis is, there is *recovery*; there is hope after all hope is gone."

And, no doubt, no small part of that recovery is the memory of the last words of their son, Steve.

"Dad, this is all in God's hands."

Even Little Hearts are Helped

Much less dramatic, but no less of a lesson for us, is the story of Erin, a two-year-old whose parents diligently told Bible stories to her, sang Christian songs with her, and reinforced, on a daily basis, the fact that God loved her and that Jesus died for her. It's instructive because sometimes we think children are "too young" to assimilate what we're teaching them, or, at the very least, too young to understand, and *definitely* too young to *apply* the Word to their lives. But the story of two-year-old Erin quickly dispels that notion.

Erin had to undergo a particularly painful procedure in the Emergency Room at the hospital in Cheyenne, Wyoming. While her father restrained her and the doctor on call administered care, Erin could say only one phrase, over and over. No, she did not call, "Mommy, mommy!" Nor did she scream anything else that might be expected from a tiny child. Instead, between sobs, this toddler could be heard whimpering, over and over, "Jesus loves me. Jesus loves me."

You see, dear mom and dad,with the Word of God comes the power of The Comforter, the Holy Spirit, who works through the Word to calm even the tiniest of hearts.

Recovery from the Troubles of Daily Life

One of the problems that I've counseled kids on more than any other problem has been the problem of broken relationships -- being jilted, "Dear Johned," "Dear Janed", or just plain dumped. Few experiences are more devastating than having the person you love suddenly tell you that, for no apparent reason, "It's over." I have seen the burliest of male athletes and the most beautiful college coeds reduced to uncontrollable tears following the breaking of a romantic relationship. The experience is so common that my first counseling session on the topic occurred during the first semester of my career as a university professor, and my most recent experience was an interruption during the writing of this chapter. But while most of my students have gone to pieces or have done something totally mindless-- including contemplating suicide in response to the shattering of their dreams, the experience of Tad illustrates what a young person who is taught Scripture for *Recovery* does in this common situation.

Tad was a young man who was deeply in love with a beautiful young girl who, in their final year of college, suddenly told Tad that the relationship was over, that there was no possibility that they would marry and spend their lives together as planned. Instead of freaking out on drugs, booze, or sex, or wallowing in self-pity, Tad shared two Scriptures which, he told me, "are helping me keep my act together." "Even when I'm in the pits," he said, "and even when I can't hold back the tears of frustration and disappointment, I am still comforted by what God says in Proverbs about my life's companion and my life's paths":

> Trust in the Lord with all thine heart, and lean not unto thine own understanding. In all thy ways acknowledge Him, and He shall direct thy paths. (Proverbs 3:5,6)
>
> House and wealth are inherited from fathers, but a prudent wife is from the Lord. (Proverbs 19:14)

What a contrast between Tad and scores of other students who did not have Tad's reservoir of Scripture to draw upon!

How would you want your child to react in a similar situation? Like Tad, or like the young people who have no anchor, whose lives are shipwrecked on the shoals of life, and who sink into addiction, depression, or suicide?

Another Unavoidable Conclusion

Suppose that no Scripture had been committed to memory by any of the people whose stories of faith fill these pages. Suppose that there were no spiritual reserves to draw upon. Suppose that, instead of hearing the reassuring voice of the Comforter, the Holy Spirit, speaking His assurances through Scripture, all they--and we--could do would be to look fearfully about and mumble, hopefully, that God wouldn't finally mete out and inflict upon us the punishment we deserve. Suppose that, instead of the victorious testimony of Steve Smart declaring his steadfast faith in Jesus Christ in headlines on the front page of the final edition of *The Denver Post* for the year 1981, thousands of readers would have been misled into speculating about what Smart and his companions had done wrong to make God so angry that He had decided to zap them on a mountainside in a fierce Colorado blizzard!

But that's not what happened. Instead, the hereoes of these stories were able to face adversity and to recover from tragedy. They had one thing in common. They knew the Word of God. They had memorized the word of God. And they applied it to their own lives.

Case histories numbering into the thousands could be cited in which Christians were helped in overcoming adversity by being uplifted by the sheer power of the Word of God. So, then, our third must as architects and builders of a program of discipline that can't fail should be pretty clear. Let's look at it in detail.

One "Sure Thing" We Can Count on for Our Children

We know our children are going to run into problems in their lives. In fact, we even know what kinds of problems our kids are going to experience. They may fall into immorality, including sexual misconduct, substance abuse, or some other temptation of the flesh. If that happens, they may believe that they are totally unworthy of forgiveness, and that, after all, "they are too far gone" and too irredeemable to get back on the right track. They may suffer health problems. Or financial problems. They or a loved one may face great danger. They may experience emotional pain. They may find themselves abandoned by friends, or without work. There are other problems, too, which we hope they will be able to avoid at all costs, such as war, famine, civil chaos, or religious persecution. Jesus warns us to be prepared for these eventualities, telling us that they could, indeed, appear in our our lifetime (Matthew 24).

Problems are unavoidable. They are an inescapable condition of human life. We can anticipate which problems are possible. We know that it is highly probable that the *least* we can expect our children to face are life's normal problems. We know that it is possible that they may face even worse situations. We are aware that the Scripture provides strength and power in the face of these problems.

We Can't Possibly Miss This Logical Conclusion!

If we know the things described above, then we must teach our children those Scriptures which will keep them strong, confident, and faithful in time of trouble. We must enable them to Recover. To fail in this responsibility would be child neglect of the worst kind. If your child ever faces the loss of his own child, permanent disability from an accident, rejection or abandonment by a loved one, financial devastation, or physical danger, all the hours spent learning the cheers to become the best cheerleader around, the years spent learning how to fire a perfect spiral with a football, or all the "A's" in academics will provide little comfort. Our kids can scarcely traverse the awesome darkness of the Valley of the Shadow of Death twirling a baton or dribbling a basketball. God's Word will be all that counts.

Knowledge is Power: What Our Kids Should Know:

Besides a vast array of Scripture texts, what else should our children know about God's Word? Two incidents that answer this question stand out very clearly in my mind. I remember, one day, trying to illustrate a point in a lecture by drawing an analogy about the monumental courage needed by an individual teacher in the struggle against the educational bureaucracy of the public schools. I cited the courage needed by David as he prepared to face Goliath. "David who?" queried a befuddled student. "In which school district," I was asked in all earnestness, "did David teach," and, "Who's Goliath?"

Admittedly, few students are this ignorant about the Bible. Nevertheless, I had received a rather abrupt, and somewhat humorous rebuke to my assumption that the analogy would be readily understood. This was the first time I was really aware of the abysmal ignorance of the Scriptures on the part of our so-called educated elite.

The second incident illustrates, perhaps, my own lack of awareness as well as the innocent ignorance of the person I was talking to. One of the most popular young men on the campus, a handsome athlete who had accepted Christ only a few weeks before, had been struggling in earnest prayer over a heavy problem. After he had prayed for many weeks without any apparent results, and in a mood of deep discouragement, he stopped by and unloaded his despair on me. After talking with me for about an hour or so in the autumn sunshine, he prepared to leave for football practice. Since I was eager to encourage him to be persistent in prayer and to persevere in his faith in God, I wrote down two Scripture references for him to read that night, knowing that he would, for sure, read them, since the problem was occupying all of his conscious thinking. Early the next morning, my student telephoned. The first reference, Luke 18:1-8, had been very helpful, he confided. He, like the widow in the parable who had kept bugging the judge until she got what she wanted, would continue to bombard the Lord with persistent prayer. The second reference, though, Hebrews 11, was of little help.

"I got the message that Hebrews 11 is about faith," he admitted, "but who were all those guys like Jacob, Gideon, Samson, and the rest of them?" This time, though, the question, "Doesn't everybody know?" was answered with resounding clarity. Everybody *doesn't* know. In fact, *many Christians* don't know. And the inspiring stories of "those guys," whose exploits were, to my young friend, a meaningless anthology of anonymous heroics, could not begin to apply to his life. Nor could the experiences of the great heroes of faith, facing the trials and tribulations of life, which constitute a record of the most potent and awe-inspiring sagas of faith ever recorded in history, could not even *begin* to help him, because he had never heard of them!

When your child faces a situation in which people or events conspire to destroy everything he holds precious, and when Satan launches an all-out attack on your child's faith in the midst of a life crisis, will your child draw on his knowledge of how Joseph declared with exuberant confidence after surviving crisis after crisis, *"As for you, you meant evil against me; but God meant it for good . . . " (Genesis 50:20)*? Will your son or daughter derive strength and the capacity to prevail by drawing upon knowledge of how Daniel survived the lion's den, how Moses overcame the might of the Egyptian empire, how Stephen faced death, and how other believers, armed only with their faith, *"won battles, overthrew kingdoms, ruled their people well, and received what God had promised them . . . " (Hebrews 11:33)*? Or will he be driven to the dust in despair because he was not provided with the strength of the knowledge of the God-created experience of the heroes of faith God has provided for us, because he doesn't know who "those guys" are?

Kidnapped, But Faith Provided Strength!

Consider the case of Dr. Judith Suazo Estrada, daughter of the Honduran President. She was kidnapped by leftist terrorists in Guatemala City in 1982, and held captive in isolation for nine days under threat of death.

"Thanks to prayer, I could stand the solitude," Dr. Estrada told reporters after her release. "I shall be grateful to my maternal grandmother for the spiritual education that she gave me that allowed me to bear those days."

You might think that there are very few young people who, like Dr. Estrada, are able to draw on their spiritual reserves. And maybe the examples you saw on the preceding pages, about kids who don't know the Scriptures, are depressing. So it should be pointed out that there are many very strong young people--and even little children--who not only know the Scriptures, but who share them and who live them. They are able, through the power of the Holy Spirit and their knowledge of the Word of God, to stand strong and "to shine out like beacon lights as children of God in a dark world full of people who are crooked and stubborn." (Philippians 2:15). But they didn't get that way by chance. They, like Judith Estrada, were systematically taught by someone who made the Word of God as normal and important a part of their lives as eating, sleeping, playing, and working. And if you are a single parent, draw encouragement from the example of Dr. Estrada's grandmother's influence. God will send a significant person into your children's lives to help you, if you ask Him for help.

The Conclusion is Unavoidable

Could the next must be any more obvious?

> We MUST teach our children the great faith
> stories of people who have recovered from
> adversity or from failure, so that our
> children will have powerful role models.

It is clear by now that we have a vitally significant task ahead of us. We now have four definite and unavoidable **musts**. We **must** teach memorization of Scriptures

1)   for Righteousness,
2)   for Resistance against the rampant destructiveness of the world's values, and
3)   for Recovery and strength in time of adversity or failure. And
4)   we **must** provide our children with a knowledge of the power of God provided to the great heroes and heroines of faith in the Scriptures. The example of these great stories of faith will provide our children with armaments against the teeth of spiritual death.

If we have to teach so many things, then, one more conclusion is obvious. This is not a part time job we're talking about! It's clear that the job is going to take *at least* as many hours as little league practice, gymnastic lessons, or delivering newspapers. But then another problem emerges immediately. *When* and *how* do I teach these things, since I have to work for a living, and there are only so many hours in a day?

The answer to this question isn't as tough as it seems. In the first place, we'll have unbeatable motivation, because we have the compelling power of the **musts** to contend with. We **must** teach Scripture texts, we **must** provide a foundation of knowledge to help our child grow spiritually, and we **must** realize that this job is the most important job we have--more important than sports, academics, extracurricular activities, hobbies, friends, or anything. Because the spiritual education we give our children may be the only thing that helps them survive terrifying experiences.

Suffering From The "If Onlys"

Here's one other thought to consider. We *will* spend time with our children, whether we like it or not. We'll either spend time in juvenile court, at the county jail, at the mental health center, with school officials, or in bitter remorse, looking back at how we could have prevented the agony we are experiencing as a result of our misplaced priorities. Or . . . we can spend time NOW, teaching them the Word of God, and ensuring that we will never need to sob, "If only . . .".

Now, just in case you're a parent who thinks it's too late to avoid the "if onlys", don't despair. It's never too late on God's calendar. There isn't enough room in this book to discuss the many, many children who turned from destructive lifestyles and became fervent followers of Christ, after their parents had all but given up on them. God honors the prayers of parents--not only prayers which ask Him to "do", but also those which ask Him to "undo" ignorance, neglect, or failure on the part of a parent.

How to avoid the "If onlys" by deciding *what* to teach and *how* to teach it is the subject of another chapter. But before we get to that chapter, let's look at the last of The Four Rs: *Relationships.*

Chapter Eight

Teaching the Fourth R: Relationships

A Strange Conversation

What started out as "shop talk" with a Christian colleague at another university turned out to be a fascinating conversation. We were discussing the topic of "challenging experiences" and "unusual students" we'd experienced over the course of our respective careers. My friend, who is in the same field I'm in, related how he dreaded full semester courses taught in a one-week format. They run from 8 a.m. to 5 p.m. Monday through Saturday. It's tough on professors, because they have a hard time even remembering students' names, let alone anything about them. And it's hard for students, because each night, they have to study for the next day. It's really difficult to develop rapport, or any kind of personal relationship with students. It's a challenge just to get through the week. So I fully sympathized with my friend's perspective as he described his feelings on the very last day of such a class a few summers ago:

"I was probably worse than the students," he laughed. "I couldn't wait to get out of there. And then, I got hit with a totally unexpected request.

"I had just given a final exam," he said. "It was almost five o'clock on a Saturday afternoon. My exhausted students acted like liberated prisoners. You know how most students linger to say 'good-byes' or some other parting words." I nodded in agreement. "And you know how, on the last day of a one-week course, students and professors alike share one idea: 'I'm outa' here!'" We both chuckled, knowingly.

"That's why I was puzzled," my friend continued, "when a very quiet young woman, whom I knew only by her first name--Maureen--lingered over her test, until the last student had departed. As she handed in her test," he related, "Maureen asked, 'Do you have a minute? I'd like to ask you about a problem.'

My friend paused. "I was surprised, to say the least," he reflected. "In all the one-week 'marathon' courses I've ever taught, no one-- and I mean *no one*--- hangs around on the last day. I mean, they pack up their gear, and they're gone!"

I nodded, chuckling. His description was accurate!

"But, here it was, a hot July afternoon, Saturday, in an all-but-deserted building," he said, "and this student wants to talk! Anyway, with more 'Christian concern' than I felt, I told her, 'Sure. We can talk right here. Is it about your grade in this class?'

"'No,'she replied, searching for what seemed to me to be just the right words. 'I wanted to talk to you because I have a reading problem. And since this course is about teaching reading at advanced levels, I thought you might be able to help me with it.'

"I was sitting there, listening to Maureen, thinking, 'What! I can't believe this! We've been hostage to the university in this drab-looking building for almost a fifty-hour week, talking about teaching reading, and *now* this woman wants to talk about a reading problem! I don't believe it! I am whipped. Emotionally and physically drained. I've been stretching my abilities to the limit, trying to condense a course, and teach it in a way that will interest and challenge the students, and maintain the academic quality of the university. And this woman wants to talk about a *reading* problem! Now?!"

By this time, my friend was totally animated.

"Quite frankly," he declared, "I really didn't believe it. I've had enough students over the years to know that no student is so diligent that she would hang around to talk about a reading problem. So, I said to her, 'Let's find out what the problem is.' I happened to have a copy of that day's newspaper in my office, and, handing it to her, I asked her to read aloud to me.

"Without missing a beat, Maureen read, fluently, several paragraphs from the front page.

"I told her, 'It doesn't seem to me that you have much of a problem,' hoping that she'd be encouraged and decide to leave. I mean, I was tired . . .."

"So what did she do?" I prompted.

"Well, she then proceeded to tell me, 'I can decode okay, but it takes me an hour just to comprehend what's on a single page of the paper.'"

Smiling, he observed, "Now we both know that there could be several plausible reasons for a reading comprehension problem like this. But, you know,

'Something' was telling me that there was more going on here than met the eye. Quickly muttering a silent prayer for the guidance of the Holy Spirit, I decided that now was the time to think about how the Scriptures could give me guidance. A verse that came immediately to mind was, *'Out of the abundance of the heart, the mouth speaks.'* I knew that Jesus said it. In the Living Bible paraphrase, the verse goes like this: *'What is in the heart, overflows into speech.'*

The verse my friend cited is one that I personally, very heavily rely upon in any counseling situation. I believe that, if I let a person talk long enough, and if I listen carefully, what is deeply embedded in the person's heart will overflow into speech. He or she will not be able to avoid talking about it. Sometimes it will be a real tiny clue. But if we take Jesus seriously, and believe that what He says, eventually-- if we listen intently enough--we'll get some clue as to what is on a person's mind. I smiled; my friend and I really were 'on the same page'--and not only professionally!

I was really caught up in my friend's story now; I could tell, by the tone of his voice, that it was about to take an unexpected twist.

"With this Scripture as a guide," he explained, "I told Maureen, 'This is really a challenging problem. Tell me about yourself. What's your major, how long have you attended this university, what do you hope to do when you graduate, where did you grow up, and so on.'

My friend continued, smiling now, "Maureen was surprised that I was interested in her. She talked, easily, about her academic program. And then she offered, almost as an aside, some personal thoughts. 'I grew up in_____.'she said. 'I lived there for the first nineteen years of my life. I come from a dysfunctional family, and . . .."'

"Out of the Abundance of the Heart..."

I was sure, before my friend said another word, that I knew exactly what was coming next. But I didn't interrupt him. He was visibly excited.

"Wow!" he exclaimed, and I knew I couldn't have interrupted him even if I'd tried. *"Dysfunctional family!* There it was! Now we were where we had to be in our conversation. What was in Maureen's heart had, indeed, overflowed into speech. And I knew," he declared, "why Maureen needed to talk to me, even though I didn't know the specifics. So as gently as I could, because I knew the terrain would be rough, I softly invited, 'Tell me about your dysfunctional family, Maureen.'

"It wasn't necessary for me to urge Maureen to talk. The words poured out, as though they had been bottled up to the bursting point. 'My parents are just not able to process anything they don't want to hear,' she declared, her eyes brimming with tears.'

"Like what? What don't they want to hear?"

"'Three years ago at Christmas ---- that Christmas was the worst time I ever spent in my life. I went home for Christmas holidays, and spent most of the time in my room. My parents expected me to act normal--as though everything was all right. But everything wasn't all right. I couldn't sit there with my parents and my brother, exchanging gifts, pretending that things were fine, and act like we were a normal family. I couldn't stand it. My parents acted as though nothing had ever happened!'

"'What had happened, Maureen?' I asked, quietly. 'What were they trying to ignore?'

"'My brother molested me as a child!' Maureen blurted. 'And I told them at the time. And they did nothing about it!' she sobbed.

"I figured," my friend explained, "that there was no turning back, now, so even though I knew I was getting really personal, I . . . I had to continue. You've been in similar situations . . ."

"Often," I agreed. "And it's never comfortable."

With that bit of encouragement, he continued. "I asked her, 'How old were you when this happened?'

"'Six,' she told me. '. . . It took place from the time I was six, until the time I was eight.'

"'And your brother?'

"'He was nine. I don't know why, but he suddenly stopped it at age eleven. And even though I told my parents about it after I was old enough to know what had gone on, they didn't want to hear about it. Since it was no longer happening, they wanted to go on as though everything was normal. As though it never happened. And they're still acting that way today!'

"There was some pornography involved,which might have had something to do with the reading problem--" my friend conjectured,--"but that's another story," he said, abruptly stifling the urge to digress.

"Anyway, the reading problem aside," my friend continued, "I asked her, 'In what ways is this affecting you now--I mean--at this time in your life, Maureen? '

"'I can't sustain any relationships,' was her answer, and, almost as an afterthought, she added, 'I will like a guy, and he will be interested in me, and, as soon as it seems to be going somewhere, I break it off. It's extremely frustrating. I don't think I'll ever find anyone I can have a lasting relationship with . . ..'"

I felt as though I were there with my friend and Maureen as he came to the climax of the story.

"I suddenly became aware of the fact," my friend reminisced, "that the room, and the building were dead quiet as the Saturday afternoon drifted into early evening, adding to the intensity of the moment. And I knew, after seeing Maureen's anguish, that it was going to take the help of God to enable her to put her traumatic experience behind her. I had to find out where she was spiritually, so I could offer her some suggestions. But you know as well as I do that I had to ask the question carefully. We get hammered just as fast as you do when it comes to professors who confess Christ. Any explicit Christian witness in a professor-student relationship would have led to vigorous Christian-bashing by the student newspaper, and by the administration. So I approached my next question a roundabout way.

"I was absolutely convinced that Maureen needed to take some steps that are outlined in the Scriptures if she wanted to recover from her problem. I really didn't see any way around talking about it, so I forged ahead and asked her the "lead-in" question."

I had to laugh, at that point, despite the gravity of the conversation, because my friend and I had both used the device of simply asking someone, "Are you a spiritual person?" We would then use their "yes," to open the door to some Christian counsel. It worked every time, because everybody thinks he or she is "spiritual."

My friend continued, even though he was aware that I knew exactly what the "lead-in" question was: "I asked her," he said, ' Maureen, are you a spiritual person?'

"Maureen's answer made the job easy for me," he laughed. "She not only says 'yes'; she answers, 'I'm a Christian.'

"So I asked her, 'Have you ever talked to a Christian counselor about this problem?' She told me that she had talked to a counselor at a Christian camp. I was encouraged to hear that. I figured that Maureen would next tell me that the counselor had advised her to follow what Jesus said in Matthew 18. You know: what to do 'if a brother sins against you, etc.' Instead, what the counselor told her practically blew my mind."

"What do you mean?" I asked him. "What advice did she get?"

"The counselor told her," he said, shaking his head in disbelief, " 'Well, accept the fact that you will be a lesbian for the rest of your life,' and without even thinking," he confessed, "I blurted out at Maureen, 'She said *what*!?' "

My friend half-apologized, looking at me as if to explain. "I was shocked," he said, "but before I could say anything, Maureen astonished me further by telling me the rest of the so-called 'Christian counseling' she received. This is exactly what she said:

"'The counselor advised me that I should accept being a lesbian,' Maureen told me, 'she said that it would be okay, that I would never be able to have normal relationships with men, and that I should just get on with my life.'"

My friend was absolutely right in what he said next. He told Maureen how unScriptural the "advice" was, and how, as a Christian, she needed to follow Jesus' advice in Matthew 18. "Maureen," he urged, "you need to contact your brother, you need to do what Jesus says, and you need to forgive him."

"I guess I wasn't really surprised by her response," he continued. "She protested, 'I could *never* talk to him about this! Besides, he lives on the West Coast, we haven't spoken in three years, and he's an alcoholic. Not only that, at that Christmas gathering he acted as though nothing had ever happened!'

"My response," he said, "was simply, 'Maureen, if you are a Christian, you have to follow what Jesus says. Your brother sinned against you. You must confront him in as gentle a manner as you are able.' Then, I added these words, which may seem to be a strange thing to say: 'It's possible that your brother really does think that you forgot all about what happened. It's possible that he suddenly stopped molesting you when he was eleven years old because, at that point, he realized, to his dismay, that what he was doing was grossly wrong.

"Don't misunderstand," he said, as if expecting me to challenge him. "I didn't share these thoughts with her to justify or excuse her brother's behavior. I shared them because of another Scripture which had come to my mind from Proverbs; namely, *'Foolishness is bound up in the heart of a child, but discipline and the rod of correction drive it out.'* I suspected that some insight had pricked his conscience. He realized that he was doing wrong. The evidence that this is what may have occurred was that after he abruptly stopped, he never spoke of it again.

"So I told Maureen again, 'If you are a Christian-- and I believe that you are--and if you follow Jesus--and I believe that you want to--then you must do what Jesus says. There is no other option. I have no solution to offer you that is better than what God has provided. There's nothing more I can say to you.'

"By this time, Maureen and I had moved our conversation from the classroom to a stone bench in the shade of a huge cottonwood tree outside the deserted building, and, as the heat of the day began to yield to the first signs of evening descending on the campus, I ended our conversation with a promise: I told her, 'I'll call you in two weeks.'"

One thing my friend emphasized was that he really had not wanted to spend time with Maureen on that late Saturday afternoon. He wanted to go home. I totally empathized with him. I could almost feel the total lack of energy to listen to anyone's personal problems, or to linger in a deserted building. He also had deliberately moved the physical setting of the conversation outside, because he thought it imprudent to be alone in an office with a young coed. But he confessed that his primary reason was that he also thought that, if they walked outside, they could get the conversation over with faster, and he might still have time to get a little recreation in before the evening was totally shot. It was almost humorous--he wanted to be sure that I understood that he didn't have a "holy" attitude, a self-sacrificing Christian spirit, or some marvelous personal insight. And I'm telling you about

111

it because what ultimately happened shows that God can use even our reluctant service and our limited talents to achieve wonderful results.

He did call Maureen after two weeks. There were a couple of seconds of bewildered silence, he said, because it took her a moment to get over the shock that a professor would actually follow up on a promise that he would call. Almost immediately, though, she then declared that she had considered his advice, and that she had decided that it was quite impossible to do what he asked her to do, but "thanks, anyway, for listening to me." He did the best he could to encourage her, but he admitted that he had a hard time sounding positive, because he was quite disappointed. He truly believed that the Bible held the answers to Maureen's problems, and that, as long as she followed advice contrary to what it said, she would never find a lasting solution to her problem, and he again told her so. Then, he related, they exchanged some sentiments along the line of "It was nice knowing you," or something like that, and ended their conversation.

"I was crestfallen," he sighed. "I fully expected that I would never hear from Maureen again. I also admit that I felt ashamed that I hadn't been more willing to spend time listening to her on that long Saturday afternoon. But here's another twist to the story: on the last day of classes, I was surprised to find in my campus mailbox a letter from Maureen. I don't remember why I decided to save it, but save it I did. And even today, when I try to read Maureen's letter aloud, I almost cry. Here's what she wrote:"

Dear Professor _____:

Since I talked to you last, my life has changed dramatically. I feel that I need to thank you for all the time and concern you shared with me. Your willingness to listen and give guidance has made a deep impression on me. The encouragement you gave me during one of the most difficult times in my life will travel with me always. Knowing that someone believes makes a remarkable difference in being able to really pursue what at times, seems impossible.

On August 10, I confronted my brother over the phone about the incest issues of the past. He admitted freely that he had violated me as a child and asked for my forgiveness. My heart opened up to him immediately when I heard those words. I never thought that he might not have known better, until you mentioned that possibility to me.

I have since told my parents about this episode. As always, they can't express their feelings toward such emotional issues. However, I will keep trying to give and receive love in this particular relationship.

I feel fortunate to have had a wonderful caring teacher as yourself. This past summer opened my eyes to a different world. I'm not exactly sure what is out there waiting for me yet, but I love surprises. Once again, thank you for your generosity.

Love,

Maureen

People Problems: God's Solutions

God's advice to us is always effective. That's as clear as can be in the story of Maureen. Here's what her story shows. My friend puts it this way:

1.   Maureen thanked a "wonderful and caring" professor--but my friend admitted that his attitudes most assuredly were not those of a wonderful and caring professor. His experience with Maureen taught me that even though God would like our best, He will use us even when we are weak. He took the time to listen to Maureen--even though he didn't really have his heart in it--because the Bible tells us, "*All look after their own interests, not those of Jesus Christ.*" *(Philippians 2: 21),* and "*Each of you, don't be interested in your own things, rather, in the things of others.*"*(Philippians 2:4) (AAT)* He knew that, as a follower of Jesus, he had an obligation put his own interests on "hold", and to be concerned about someone else.

2.   Jesus taught us that the Holy Spirit would "remind us" of what we have learned from the Word. The Bible is loaded with advice about "people problems." If we study the Word, the Holy Spirit can "remind" us of what we have learned. And what we learn about people problems can be applied. Consider this:
>   The Holy Spirit brought to mind the verse, "*What is in the heart overflows into speech.*"

114

Putting that verse into practice opened the
door to what was bothering Maureen.
> Matthew 18 gave Maureen foolproof advice
for approaching her brother. When she
followed what Jesus ordered us to do,
blessings followed. Blessings would have
followed even if no reconciliation had taken
place. Why? Because Jesus also told his
disciples, "*You know these things, now do
them. That is the path of blessing.*"
> What the Book of Proverbs has to say about
what goes on in the minds of children
provided insight into Maureen's brother's
possible motivation for never talking about
what had happened. It was the Bible that
provided the insight. It had nothing to do
with the fact that my friend is aprofessor,
or that he was drawing upon experience, or
any other worldly wisdom.

Other Guidelines from God

There's one lecture I never fail to deliver to my
Teacher Education students. I tell them how to
absolutely, positively guarantee that they will get into
trouble. I then give them example after example of
outstanding teachers who got into trouble, who had
diffficulties with parents, who were reprimanded by

administrators, or who worried about being sued. All because they either didn't know, or didn't apply, what the Bible says about the tongue. They said what they shouldn't have said. They revealed confidential information, or slandered a colleague. Maybe they disparaged a department head, belittled a child, or "told tales out of school." I tell my students that they will see, in at least one university classroom, a professor who will "pray" to his students. I then get down on my knees at the front of the room, I look them in the eye, and I implore them, "Please, please, please. Keep your mouth shut!"

Now, for a child schooled in the Scriptures, the advice has already been learned. James talks about how the tongue is a deadly fire, and goes on to illustrate how much damage careless gossip can do. Solomon describes a person who has a faithful spirit as one who can keep a secret. Paul talks about the harmful effects of slander, gossip, and backbiting. He also advises Christians to "say only what gives a blessing."

A child who knows the Scriptures has the wisdom to know what to say and what not to say, when to speak, and when to remain silent. The Word of God will be a light for his path. Such a child will never get into trouble by saying what should not be said.

Other Examples of Practical Common-Sense Advice

There is enough common-sense advice in the Bible to fill several books. In fact, in one of the author's other books, *Guaranteed Steps to Managing Stress,* a whole chapter is devoted to how to avoid stress of people problems by following God's advice. There is advice on what to do when you are placed into a situation where two people have conflicting stories about what allegedly happened. There is advice about what jealousy will do to you. There's advice about quarreling, about lending money, about how to work, about what to devote your time and energy to, about how to recognize whether a person can be depended upon. There's advice about drinking alcohol, about sexual behavior, about how to handle failure, including your own failure.

The list could go on and on. Many of the verses in the list at the end of this book have to do with just plain living--with living successfully, happily, and triumphantly.

A Continuing Mystery

One characteristic of the late 90s was an abundance of "advice" features in the print and electronic media, featuring a gaggle of gurus of every description, doling out advice on every problem imaginable. Some people paid good money to call "psychics" for expensive pay-by-the-minute "guidance" on how to live their lives. Others let it all hang out in public, and revealed the most intimate details of their personal and private lives on television or on radio, anxiously searching for some sanity in their mixed-up world.

Some of the most ungodly, foolish, and destructive advice possible was dispensed, like an emotional antibiotic, by "experts" who conveyed an air of authority and confidence. However, their advice, especially in areas bearing upon sexual behavior, was diametrically opposed to the Bible.

It also became the rage to label as "spiritual" any activity that tried to tap into nature, one's "inner self", or any out- of -the- ordinary experience, whether it had anything to do with God or not.

Here's what absolutely amazes me: People will listen to so-called "experts" in family life whose own families are in disarray. They will listen to "relationship" counselors who have been married and divorced several times. They will be deceived by false definitions of love. They will ignore the plain words of the Bible, and read "self-help" books which present advice which any Christian can see is virtually guaranteed to be self-destructive. And they will reject what the Scriptures have to say, without ever reading the Bible!

In my files are medical reports from a variety of professional sources, identifying certain physical and emotional illnesses. The reports discuss how physical illnesses are made worse, how they sometimes begin, and how people can actually speed up their healing. In every case, without exception, the Bible has something to say about which human behaviors are associated with certain medical conditions. In fact, there is even a section, in *Guaranteed Steps to Managing Stress,* entitled, "The Latest Research: Three Thousand Years Old!"

Hidden Messages--But Children Who Have Wisdom Will Not Be Deceived

The list of verses at the end of this book, having to do with Relationships, will show very clearly how our children can be guided by God's Word in relating to other people. One illustration that sticks out in my mind, though, occurred recently, when I "happened" upon an eleven-year-old Christian girl busily communicating on the Internet. I could see that she was responding to a survey, so I asked her whether I might read what she had written. What was asked of her in the survey--and how she responded, without any prompting--thrilled me! Obviously, her parents had been putting into practice discipline that can't fail. They had imbued their daughter with wisdom beyond her years.

The Internet site was a popular site for kids: Nickelodeon. Now, in the case of this child, she was using a "protected" Internet Service Provider. It's a Christian company called *Integrity on Line*, which does a good job of screening out offensive material, and which protects kids from getting on to any site or any material which could be harmful to them. But even the most professionally-polished provider can't screen out subtle messages like the one young Jillian responded to.

Here's what Nickelodeon asked, and here's the gist of what Jillian wrote in response.

Question: Who embarrasses you more, your parents, or your grandparents?

Can you see the hidden message in the question? A young child who accesses this site is given a message: "My parents, or my grandparents, should be an embarrassment to me." The message plants the seeds of disrespect. In the Book of Proverbs, Solomon tells children to honor the elderly. Elsewhere, children are told to obey and honor their parents. On the Nickelodeon site, however, the message is that parents and grandparents are "embarrassing". The next logical conclusion is that they must be doing something stupid. Therefore, they are not worthy of respect.

When I read Jillian's response, I could have hugged her! But then, I thought, "Jillian's parents are the ones who should be hugged! They are raising a woman of discretion and wisdom. " Below the question, Jillian had responded:

"This question is not an appropriate question for a children's Website. God tells us, 'Honor your father and your mother, that it may be well with you, that thou mayest live long on the earth.' Neither my parents nor my grandparents embarrass me. They are all wonderful people who are part of a wonderful family. You owe your readers an apology."

Sincerely,

Jillian , _____@_____lolusa.com

Relationships and Resistance Rolled into One

The Website Jillian visited conveyed a powerfully destructive message. Ninety-nine per cent of children visiting the website will internalize the message. It will become a part of their value system. It will affect the way they will look at their parents or grandparents. It will affect their behavior. It will affect how they obey. And it will affect their well-being. They do not have the training to Resist the subtle, satanic undertones. (And I do not use the word "satanic" carelessly!) Like the children in the chapter on Resistance, they will be blinded by a fog which they never see, and which they will never recognize. They will suffer negative consequences, because their "automatic pilot" did not kick in. Their parents will not have protected them with God's Word.

In Jillian's case, though, the Holy Spirit, <u>through the Word of God she learned,</u> brought to mind a Scripture text which helped her Resist the destructive message. It was a verse which had to do with Relationships. She was--and will be--protected from negative influences because she was thoroughly taught--disciplined--in the Four Rs, and because in this instance, she applied Scriptures having to do with two of the Four Rs.

Applying the Word of God to Relationships Problems

In the chapter *Getting Down to Specifics: What, When, and How to Do It,* the ways to teach Scriptures and stories which have to do with relationships are outlined. It's important to remember, though, that any time a "people" problem comes up, there's an opportunity to apply what the Bible says. Of course, that means that *parents* must know what the Word of God says.

So let's conclude this section with some suggestions. First, study the Word yourself, especially the Book of Proverbs. If you go only that far, you'll find tons of verses that give guidance on relationships. If you want more, go to Matthew 18, Matthew 5, and Galatians 6. If you want more than that, start learning, for yourself, the verses at the back of this book that have to do with relationships.

Once you know a whole array of verses that bear upon relationships, start listing situations in which various verses apply. For example, if you're in a disagreement with someone, and you're tempted to snap back, try to think of a verse that applies. A verse such as, "A soft answer turns away a person's wrath, but harsh words stir up anger," will come to your mind. Follow the advice in the verses. Then, whenever you can, try to bring a Scripture verse to bear upon what you and your children see--at the grocery store, driving here and there, at the playground, and so on. You'll be surprised how many opportunities there are to apply the Scriptures to "relationships" problems.

One More Thing: What About The Peer Group ?

The Bible repeatedly and emphatically warns against associations with the wrong kinds of people. My professional experience has totally validated what the Bible says. Therefore, I cannot possibly overstate what I'm going to say next: *Parents, we must absolutely, completely, positively, and unhesitatingly take unflinching control over whom we allow our kids to associate with.* We must know who our kids' friends are, what their friends are like, and what their friends' parents believe and value. We must *totally control* our children's friendships. After all, even we, as adults, conform to some influences of our various peer groups. Then how on earth can we ignore the fact that our children will be likely to be influenced! And if God warns us--as mature adults--to avoid certain relationships, how on earth can we not apply the same level of seriousness to the relationships our kids have!

A Closing Thought

Our task is intimidating. But don't be afraid of it. God will equip you to do an outstanding job. Read the Word. Pray for guidance. And remember what Jesus promised: *"The Comforter, the Holy Spirit . . . will remind you of everything I told you."* John 14:26).

A Quiz on the Four Rs
(Righteousness, Resistance, Recovery, Relationships)

The quiz which follows contains a number of statements Christian kids commonly hear. On the university campus, in particular, Christian students are consistently confronted with arguments and challenges by unbelieving students and professors.

Our children can defend themselves against a relentless assault on their faith only if they are thoroughly grounded in the Word. For example, your children should be able to respond to, say, item number 20 on the quiz, by citing Scripture verses such as *"cast not your pearls before swine,"* or *"give not that which is holy unto the dogs"* because Jesus tells us that we may be "torn to pieces." In other words, they should know that there are some situations in which there is such hostility to the Word that discretion dictates that we wait for a better opportunity.

It is also true that if our children try to come up with an intellectual response to hostile arguments or personal problems they will face, they may be likewise be "torn to pieces." The only reliable response to temptation, trouble, guilt, or broken relationships is God's Word. (Ephesians 6: 11-17).

Even Michael the archangel didn't try to argue when accosted by Satan. He used God's Word for a defense. He declared, simply, *"The Lord rebuke you!"* (Jude 9.)

The quiz has been used with Christian school teachers as a guideline to show real-life applications of Scripture that we ought to be teaching to children.

Directions: **For each statement, cite a Scripture verse or a Bible character or story that provides God's answer to the statement.**

1. "We all worship the same God. We just have different ways of getting to heaven."

    Response:_____

    _____

2. "I think _____ went to heaven when he died. He was a great guy who really helped a lot of people."

    Response:_____

    _____

3. "Times have changed. We have new knowledge and and new information. We know that it's just natural that people need sex, whether they're married or not. God understands."

    Response:_____

    _____

4. "Hey, the Bible says we're saved by faith, so I'm forgiven, right? So I can do whatever I want, and just repent."

Response _____

_____

5. "Well, people are born neutral, or good. So to say that a baby is sinful is ridiculous!"

Response:_____

_____

6. "So, if you party a bit, and get a little high, who gets hurt? God wants us to be happy."

Response:_____

_____

7. "If two people don't get along, divorce is ok in God's eyes, as long as they mutually agree to part."

Response:_____

_____

8. "I get so scared when_____."

Response: _____

_____

9. "I'm really worried about _____.
Sometimes I wonder whether God
is in control."

Response:_____

_____

10. "Do you think God really cares about
each person's needs?"

Response:_____

_____

11. "I'm worried about what's going to
happen tomorrow, or next month, when . . ."

Response:_____

_____

12. "To me, religion is a private thing.   It's
wrong to try to push your religion onto
somebody else.

Response:_____

_____

13. "Boy, are you narrow-minded!

Response:_____

_____

14. "God said He'd protect us, so get off my case. I'm not afraid to take chances. God will protect me."

Response:_____

_____

15. "If you had obeyed God, you wouldn't be having these problems."

Response:_____

_____

16. "You'll always get exactly what you pray for. God said so."

Response:_____

_____

17. "You don't have to go to church or a Bible study group or places like that, to worship. I find God in the mountains."

Response:_____

_____

18. "To believe in something like creation, or the Flood, defies natural logic."

Response:_____

_____

19. "No truly educated person could believe
in a virgin birth, a physical resurrection,
or stuff like that."

Response:_____
_____

20. "I know Professor Cynic constantly shreds
Christians who quote the Bible in his classes,
but I think you ought to quote it anyway."

Response:_____
_____

21. "You wouldn't believe the dirty stuff
they are pulling on me behind my back.
They're out to ruin me!"

Response:_____
_____

22. "I don't see anything wrong with just looking at skin
flicks, or R or X-rated movies."

Response:_____
_____

23. "My friend goes to this psychic, and, like, he
says you can find out what major you should `
take, and stuff."

Response:_____
_____

24. "It's ridiculous to think that God could forgive a monster like Jeffrey Dahmer, or terrorists who kill innocent people."

Response:_____

_____

25. "I loved (him/her) so much! How could God let (him/her) break off with me?"

Response:_____

_____

Answers can be found in Appendix C, staring on page 246.

Appendix A, starting on page 241, lists Scripture texts that apply to the quiz.

Chapter Nine

Getting Down To Specifics:
What, When, And *How* To Do It

There are probably two times during a day that are "prime time" for teaching God's Word and God's ways: mealtime, and bedtime. With very little effort and with God's help we can achieve superb results in spiritual training at these times. Let's say, for example, that the family gets together at suppertime. The *rock-bottom minimum* that can be done would be that the meal would begin with a prayer. Not a "canned" prayerbook prayer, although that'll do if you're just beginning, but a prayer which is a genuine reflection of family concerns. Let's look at this activity a little closer:

Activity	Specifics	Time
Prayer before meal and after meal.	Ask God to bless the food and the family. Take turns saying or reading the prayer.	1 minute

131

Parents' Role	Child's Role
Be an example. Offer the prayer. Teach the children by example. (Even the disciples said, "Teach us to pray.")	From time to time say or read the prayer.

Main Things Learned:

(1) You are building a habit--a habit so strong that it will seem as awkward to eat without praying as it would be to eat mashed potatoes and gravy without a plate. Something important and vital to the meal will be missing, if it doesn't begin with a prayer.

(2) You are teaching your child that you are obedient to God, that you are concerned about things spiritual, and that God hears our prayers.

(3) You are providing practice for your child in praying. You are making prayer a natural part of his life.

You are accomplishing all of these important teachings in *one minute of each day!* That's about as much time as it takes to locate the jar of vitamins in the cupboard, get a glass of water, and have a child take a vitamin tablet. Even the Lord's Prayer, prayed slowly and deliberately, takes only twenty-three seconds!

Whatever work you do, and however hard your work, anybody can take *one minute* to teach the three major lessons mentioned above each day.

But let's took a little closer at what could go on at mealtime or at bedtime. One of the main services we can perform for one another is to talk to one another or to listen to one another. I can remember, for example, how frustrated I would often get at the university when I had no classes, meetings, or appointments scheduled, and when my eagerly-anticipated time to catch up on some studying or research tasks would be taken by a student who stopped by "just to talk." I never minded at all missing a lunch hour or other free time to listen to a student who had a problem, but to spend the time "just to talk" seemed to be a frivolous waste of time. But one day I realized that having nobody to talk to or nobody to listen to was as potentially serious as any problem I would listen to, and that it was extremely important to young people to have somebody to talk to. As a matter of fact, many, if not most of the people I have listened to who have had marital problems have identified this very factor, an absence of communication, as the chief cause of their marriage breakdown. It's the same problem--nobody to talk to or nobody who will really listen--that leads the lonely shut-in retiree to dial the time and temperature or to call the radio talk show just to speak to or listen to another human voice whose focus is seemingly personal. And what causes the young, bored, married person to become "involved" in an adulterous relationship? Not sex. Not money. Not excitement. Certainly not a new social circle. *Communication.* Talking and listening. Appreciating someone else. Or, as the Apostle Paul puts it in his letter to the Philippians, *"Don't just think about your own affairs, but be interested in others, too, and what they are doing"* (Phil. 2:4) (TLB).

133

That brings us to step two in the Christian education in your home. Again, you spend almost no extra time, but the lessons will be terrific. It looks like this on a teacher's lesson plan:

Activity

Talking and listening at mealtime and/or bedtime

Specifics

The easiest way to get the ball rolling, if you haven't done this before, is to give each person a chance to talk about what was "the funniest," "the best," the "worst," or the "most interesting" thing that happened that day. Or be even more casual, and "just talk."

Time

Mealtime, no extra time spent, although there are some ground rules. Don't answer the phone at mealtime. Unplug it if you can. No "world or local news" on T.V., because you'll miss your family's news. No T.V. news is as important as your daughter's first part in a play, or your son's first varsity game.

Parent's Role & Child's Role

Talking and Listening

first part in a play, or your
son's first varsity game.

    Some of these things are tough to get used to. The morning paper, before we had children, was as important to the flavor of my meal as the salt and pepper, and it was tough not to read at the table, but we no longer ignore each other, buried behind the newspaper. Consider this for a minute. How much talking and listening and sharing and caring can go on during a meal if, during the meal, parents and children are accepting telephone calls, gulping food down to leap from the table to run off with neighborhood kids, or if the television is blaring away with news or entertainment, or if part of the family is munching away on meat, potatoes, and the sports page or the comics? And I have been a "guest" in homes where all these things are going on, all at the same time! Imagine a celebration of Christmas dinner taking place under these circumstances. No, on second thought, that's a lousy example, because it's likely that a football game would be on television. Well, imagine, instead, the Last Supper being interrupted with a disciple saying, "Telephone, Master." Ridiculous? No more so than a family who probably gather where they can talk and listen and share with one another for only a half hour each day as a unit--a total of 3 1/2 hours a week, or, to look at it another way, a grand total of 3094 hours. That's only about 129 days in a seventeen-year-old's life span before he leaves home!
    That family allows telephones and appointments and television and the newspaper and lots of other

unimportant and distracting trivia destroy the opportunities for communication available during these 3,094 hours. Opportunities that could be open for building trust, confidence, faith, and spiritual strength.

Main things learned by talking and listening:

(1)   You are teaching your children that you are vitally interested in them and in what they are doing. You are teaching them that you will listen with interest to what they have to say. This particular fact is extremely important.

If your children will communicate openly with you, they will not have to seek counseling elsewhere.

In the first place, if they can share successes and failures with you, that might provide catharsis, or outlet for them. Then, some incident that might have become a problem if they had not had a chance to talk about it will not become a problem at all.

If your children can talk freely to you, they will not have to carry their burdens alone. They will not go to bed at night and wrestle with their worries.

Your children will also have their values reinforced by you. And they will develop the habit of looking to you, first, for advice, no matter what the problem they happen to be struggling with at the time.

Don't Let the Blind Lead the Blind

In the second place, if your children don't have to seek counseling elsewhere, they won't receive impractical advice, or worse than that, destructive advice. What is the likelihood that your child will receive good counseling when he or she seeks it from peers? Will the peer group support *your* ideas? Will your child's friends side with the teachers, or with you, in a child-teacher or child-parent dispute? Will the advice be spiritual, wise, and mature? You already know the answer to that one. And I can assure you, from personal experience with high school and college counselors, that professional counselors are no better. In fact, they may be dangerously worse, because their status as "counselors" who work in a "counseling center" or "guidance office" lends an aura of credibility to them and respectability to their advice, which, at the least, is often foolish, and sometimes, dangerous. Need examples? Okay. In an earlier chapter we met Sarah. Remember her? She was the one who went from biofeedback to human sensitivity to meditation therapy seeking fulfillment. What was her most recent job? Hang onto your hat. Counselor. Worse yet, she was hired as a live-in counselor for a group of "troubled" students at a summer retreat program. How do I know? Because I personally contacted the director to attempt to persuade him to find other employment for Sarah within the camp structure. But she was nevertheless hired as a counselor. Maybe her job helped her find "fulfillment." It's almost ludicrously analogous to allowing someone to perform surgery, not because he's

137

qualified, but because he's "always wanted to be a surgeon," and it could help him find fulfillment.

I also know a full time counselor with a Ph.D. who is a counselor in a major university in the Midwest who deliberately and with malicious intent, set out to destroy a rival's reputation because the rival had professionally upstaged him in public. The counselor was an expert in interpersonal relations--on how to achieve harmony in the workplace!

Still another parent-and-family counselor's child told me, publicly, in a discipline seminar, "Dr. Burron, I do not get along with my father. We have not spoken in several months. He left my mother, and my brother and I do not get along with him." His area of expertise? Parenting. He is a licensed marriage and family counselor!

Public institutions *cannot* provide spiritual counseling. They provide "options," some of which might be irreconcilably opposed to the teachings of Jesus Christ. They also provide "non directive counseling." That's counseling in which the counselor "facilitates" problem-solving by eliciting conversation from the counselee without ever passing judgment on what is said. The idea of direct guidance, or criticism, is totally unacceptable to many professional counselors.

The lesson that you teach by mealtime conversation pays huge dividends on a very small investment of time. You can head off some problems completely, you can limit some problems before they become serious, and most important of all, you can share the solutions and the guidance provided by the Holy

138

Spirit. The first major lesson is extremely far-reaching. Let us now look at lessons number two and three:

(2)   You are teaching your children that they can share their failures, as well as their successes with you. You will be developing a habit of open communication.

(3)   You are teaching your children to be interested in one another. They will learn to become good listeners, as well as honest communicators. And as you do these things, sharing successes, failures, joys, and sorrows, you will be amazed to discover that your children will share their problems with you, and that you can provide Spirit-guided counsel as you share solutions which are based on the Word of God. The Word of God will become, for your children, a real source of power with obvious applicability to daily living, because you will be able to relate God's Word to real events in their lives, not to hypothetical situations created for a Sunday school lesson.

At this point, let's consider a couple of facts. So far, two activities have been recommended as an answer to the question of *what* and *when* to teach and *how* to teach it. The two activities we have seen teach six concepts which can help produce powerful people who can lead outstanding lives:

(1)   Prayer habit
(2)   Faith in prayer
(3)   Practice in prayer
(4)   Open communication
(5)   Confidence in parents as trusted friends
(6)   Interest in others.

The Most Amazing Fact of All

Let's consider the most amazing fact of all. The six major concepts are instilled by adding only *one minute* to your mealtime routine and by changing some very easily-altered mealtime activities!

So far, the first two activities that have been suggested--praying and having mealtime conversation--are not hard to do. If you are a reader who has typically begun meals with a prayer of thanks, and who uses mealtime as a sharing time, you know that no meal is complete without these activities and that they are not at all a chore. If you haven't done these things from the time that your children were preschoolers, mealtime is the best time to do them, since it would be awkward to suddenly try to initiate a bedtime conversation with a teenager. Mealtime is a natural time to converse, and now is the time to begin. Remember that the Holy Spirit will bless your efforts. You know that even if it's tough at first, and even though you may well eat your meals in awkward silence for a while, with the help of God you will succeed. It is also important to remember that it is not up to you to make your child responsive to the prayer and to the mealtime conversation time. That's the Holy Spirit's responsibility. Your responsibility is to provide the best conditions possible within which the Holy Spirit can work. Creating a change of heart and attitude is His job. If you have small children, or if you have habitually and faithfully pursued the activities described above since your children were little, the next activity, discussed below, will be just as natural for you to do as the first two. It will become as important a part of mealtime as the food itself. On the other hand, if you haven't habitually done this next activity, it'll be tough. But again, remember that your job is not to create faith. Your job is to teach and to provide the conditions and the nourishment in which faith can grow. So, with the help of God, the next activity can become as important and helpful to all the members of your family as the prayer before the meal and the conversation during the meal.

Before we look at the activity, I should say that I know all about the kid who, as a thirteen-year old, "looks right through" his parents, or the child who, at ten, is insistent about watching his television show on time after supper, or the child who sullenly gobbles his food and then glares at his plate in impatience to leave, or the one who brings up baseball practice, homework, friends, or a myriad of other reasons for getting supper over with. Pay no attention. Provide the conditions. Do what God says and the Holy Spirit will create changes.

God knocked a belligerent and fanatical Pharisee off his horse as he zealously pursued the persecution of Christians. God changed Saul into Paul, the greatest evangelist since Jesus Christ. God provided a huge fish to swallow an obstinate prophet in order to provide transportation for the prophet to preach to the throngs in a place where He wanted the prophet to go. A rebellious Jonah preached his heart out! If God did those things, rest assured that He can open the heart and the mind of a sullen teenager who "can't wait" to join the fanatical throngs at the local roller rink or the mall.

Great Americans of the Past Did This Activity

Let's take a look now at this tough activity, and at who does what. And let's look at what happens as a result when we do it.

Activity	Specifics
Reading and discussing the Scripture.	For young children read Bible stories from Bible story books. Often, the Bible story will have a verse which accompanies each story. For older children, read selected portions of the Living Bible. Start with stories in the Gospels. Use the parables if you know their interpretation. Read the book of Acts. Read the Epistles, 10-15 verses, at most.

Time

3-5 minutes *at most*. Discussion may take *a few* extra minutes. Usually, a story can take longer, but an instructional reading such as is found in the Epistles, should be quite brief.

Parents' Role

Read. Explain. Ask children to restate, in their own words, what has been read.

For younger children, ask questions about pictures, or ask "fact" questions about what they recall from the story. For older children, ask questions like, "What do you think this means?"

Child's Role

Read when asked. Listen. Ask questions. Answer questions. (If children are reluctant to answer, use "multiple choice" type questions, such as, "Do you think that such-and-such, or do you think thus-and-so?") Get them to pick an answer.

Main Things Learned

(1) ". . . *Man shall not live by bread alone, but by every word that proceedeth out of the mouth of God.*" *(Matthew 4:4)* Children will learn the fact that the Word of God is a necessary and indispensable part of our daily lives-- spiritual food, the Bible implies--which is necessary for us to grow spiritually.

(2) The habit of reading Scriptures daily will be acquired.

(3) Spiritual growth will take place. God promises this.
" . . . *like newborn babies, thirst for the pure milk of the Word, so that you'll grow till you're saved."* (I Peter 2:2, AAT)

(4) Naturally, the Scriptures will be learned, but accompanying this growth in knowledge will be a growth in positive attitudes. Repeated use of the Scripture will lead to familiarity with the Scripture, so that your child will never feel self-conscious or inadequate in sharing God's Word with others.

(5) Increased knowledge of the Scripture will give your child more and more of God's kindness and peace, more ability to lead a good life, a greater capacity to withstand and overcome even the most negative of influences, and the capacity to relate well with other people, as well as increased ability to be useful to Jesus Christ. All these gifts are promised in 2 Peter 1: 1-8!

Avoiding Overkill

Notice that, in the discussion on what to do and when to do it, there has been an emphasis on *being brief*. You can afford to be brief, because if you believe what you've read so far, you know that you'll be diligently and habitually doing the recommended activities almost every day, because you know that you **must** do them, not that you **should** do them. So you'll have time for a lot of lessons, and a lot of review.

There is a second reason, equally practical, for brevity. The average attention span of a listener, when no visual aids are available, is very limited. I am acutely aware of this fact as a university professor; therefore, whether I am teaching undergraduate students or advanced graduate students, extensive use is made of visual aids. This requires that students copy portions of the aids, take notes, or react orally. Even with the requirement of active participation, and even though students say that the instructor is not difficult to listen to, I am still aware of students' minds drifting off to matters of more immediate concern to them. Consider this, also. *The Parable of the Talents,* presented in Luke 19, takes less than one minute to tell. It was one of Jesus' main sermons. Together, the *Parable of the Persistent Widow* and the *Parable of the Pharisee and the Publican* take less than 90 seconds to tell. They, too, constitute two major sermons of the Lord Jesus.

Much can be accomplished in a very few minutes. Surprisingly, you may find, to your delight, that if you teach your children to share the responsibility of reading the Scripture, you may have to keep *them* from becoming too long-winded. Surprisingly, too, some of the most in-depth discussions we've had in our own home after our mealtime Scripture readings have followed the sharing of only one verse!

Some Additional Benefits

One of the most fascinating aspects about the Scripture is that, although its focus is on how we will grow and prosper and be healthy spiritually, some other unusual benefits result when we follow what God says. For example, Jesus says, *"Seek ye first the kingdom of God and His righteousness, and all these things shall be added unto you"* (Matthew 6:33). The book of Proverbs describes another unusual benefit, advising us that, *"When a man's ways please the Lord, he makes even his enemies be at peace with him"* (Proverbs 16:7).. In other words, his enemies will not be able to make any kind of a valid case against him.

But There Are Even More Fringe Benefits!

Most parents will be thrilled and delighted to discover that, by following the regular practice of reading and discussing the Bible with their children, a most unexpected benefit will be derived. They will improve the *academic* achievement of their children!

One of the most interesting discoveries of research in the field of reading achievement is that, while achievement scores in reading are up, achievement in one vital area of reading--comprehension--has declined. Specifically, researchers have isolated one particular type of reading comprehension in which achievement has dropped: inferential comprehension. That's the ability to draw logical conclusions about what is only implied in a piece of writing. And which type of comprehension is *the* main type required when the parables and many other Scriptures are read? Inferential comprehension! In the area of reading, again, one of the factors most highly related to achievement in reading comprehension and to success in other academic subjects is the factor of vocabulary knowledge. And how is a child exposed to challenging vocabulary terms beyond the limits of his own experiences? By reading and discussing challenging material in a non-threatening environment. What is more challenging than the Scripture? What is a more non-threatening environment than a home in which the love of Jesus Christ is systematically taught and practiced?

While we're at it, let's look at still another fringe benefit which results from sharing the Scriptures with your children. Your child will attain a more thorough understanding of art, music, and literature as a result of his understanding of the Scriptures. For instance, here are just a very few examples of great achievements of gifted individuals in the arts which are either based on Scripture or which make extensive allusions to the Bible:

Da Vinci: "The Last Supper"
Steinbeck: "The Pearl"
Handel: "The- Messiah"
Melville: "Moby Dick" (Ishmael, Ahab, and Elijah)
Dali: "Christ of St. John of the Cross"
MacLeish: "JB"

Shakespeare, who is encountered by most students in reading or literature classes, used more than 1,200 quotations or references from the Bible.

The background knowledge provided by the Bible is absolutely essential to the literal comprehension of art, music, and literature. Indeed, this fact is one of the main reasons used to justify courses in "Bible" in the public schools. Whole volumes have been written about how references from the Bible have influenced law, politics, art, music, and so on.

Improved academic achievement in school will be a result of spiritual training! Children who are raised in Christian homes are often high achievers not only because they value achievement and attempt to utilize their talents to glorify Christ; they are high achievers because their spiritual blessings have been accompanied by intellectual growth and background knowledge in literal comprehension, inferential comprehension, oral expression, and vocabulary development. As an educator, I recommend to all parents that they do a thorough study and discussion of the Old and New Testaments with their children. It's one of the most effective ways to develop advanced oral and written expression. It improves literal and inferential comprehension! It teaches eloquence in public speaking.

Academic fringe benefits are desirable, but obviously they are not the most important or compelling reason to study the Scriptures. The goal of Scripture study is to make our children "wise unto salvation"; that is, to help them to "shine out like beacon lights" through faith in Jesus Christ. The most effective way to do this is to equip them with the power which will keep the lights shining, no matter how dark the situation. Bible stories and Bible knowledge unquestionably provide power, but the most effective, irresistible, incredible power which keeps the light shining in the face of temptation is the power of the *memorized* word of God.

An earlier example pointed out that when Satan tempted Jesus, Jesus responded by saying, "*It is written. . .*" What wasn't pointed out in the example was that even

Satan realized the awesome power of the Word in his attempt to tempt Jesus. Satan tried to appeal to Jesus with a verbatim quotation from the Scripture!

One example of how the mighty power of the Word of God sustains Christians not only when they are in physical danger, but also when their faith is challenged, concerns a professional colleague of mine. During a period of time when it was just beginning to become acceptable to publicly derogate Christians, a Christian philosophy professor who attempted to provide a balanced point of view to his classes in a public university was viciously attacked by non-Christian students and colleagues alike. Students who had never violated classroom decorum disregarded university etiquette and launched biting verbal attacks during question-and-answer sessions in the professor's classes. Faculty colleagues, who should have been concerned about academic freedom, publicly maligned the professor, going so far as to agitate their students to provoke them to even further ferocity of attack. The student newspaper, in an attempt to capitalize on campus controversy, plastered the professor's picture on the front page, implying in a glaring headline that the professor's insistence in presenting an objective view of Christianity was a crime against academic freedom. Even the professor's superordinates were of no help. His department chairman remained strangely mute, and his dean, instead of defending him, publicly demanded the removal of some of his instructional materials from his classroom. The onslaught on the professor lasted for days, increasing in intensity and becoming the *"cause celebre"* of the campus. His fine reputation as a researcher, a scholar, and a teacher was totally ignored, his personal reputation was besmirched, and he was regarded with disdain by many faculty and students alike as a Jesus Freak--"that Christian" who contaminated the purity and usurped the prerogatives of academic freedom.

I knew of no one who could have stood more strongly in adversity than my friend, the philosophy professor. Nevertheless, the inexorable mounting of tension and hostility, day after day, took their toll. My friend began to look drawn and tired. He slept fitfully, if at all. He could not eat. His career was in jeopardy, his family's means of support was threatened, and his life's work ignored--buried under a mountain of ridicule and contempt. Now, at this time, how could I, as a Christian friend, help my friend? By counterattacking? Some friends tried, in the "letters" column in the student newspaper, to defend him, but with little effect. Others tried platitudes like, "hang in there," or "you know how these things are. They'll die down." I suppose I could have said, "Remember the story of Stephen; he was stoned for his beliefs, and put to death." But I'm afraid that at this time of personal and professional crisis in my friend's life, a general knowledge of Scripture or a sharing of some narrative facts of an historical account, even if we had had the opportunity for an extended conversation, would not have helped much. What was needed was a potent and explosive Scripture reference which was at once timely and succinct, and which would hit home with brilliant intensity. Something that my friend could repeat to himself. Something to cling to in the middle of the tempest raging around him. Something like this:

*When you are reviled and persecuted and lied
about because you are My followers--wonderful! Be
happy about it! Be very glad . . . (Matthew 5:11,12
TLB)*

or something equally brief, powerful, and to-the-point, like this:

*The apostles left the Council chamber rejoicing that
God had counted them worthy to suffer dishonor
for His name. (Acts 5:41 TLB)*

As it happened, the first of these Scriptures was shared with my friend by a young female colleague. The professor reflected, later, that it was a great and sustaining comfort, lifting him from the morass of anxiety and elevating him to new heights of optimism. It was one of several anchors in a storm. It was offered to him when he needed it--spontaneously, by another Christian, in a moment in which he was obviously suffering. It was a Scripture which his Christian friend had been directed to memorize as a young girl, and which had never been used by her until this precise moment! Yet, at the time it was needed, it carried with it the gift of peace of mind. It was additionally powerful because he, too, knew the verse by memory, and needed only this stimulus to recall it and to use it!

Suppose, though, that no memorization of Scripture had taken place. Imagine this. A man on the verge of tears. Distraught. Suffering from repeated nights of sleeplessness, evincing visible signs of anxiety and nervousness. Imagine, instead of a friend sharing a powerful Scripture text, a scene in which the friend says, "I know there's a verse somewhere about persecution, and I'll look it up for you if you wait. If you have to leave, I'll telephone you tonight. If I don't catch you then, I'll see you tomorrow. In the meantime, remember that there are a lot of verses in Scripture which tell us that God is with us when we're suffering."

Power in the Memorized Word

The point seems abundantly clear. Memorization of Scripture yields power. Personal power. Spiritual power. Power to help others. Power to stand strong in adversity. You, as a parent, have the priceless opportunity to build power in your children, with the guarantee that your efforts will be successful.

There are many blessings to be accrued from the memorization of Scripture, both in the area of developing personal power to persevere and to prevail against overwhelming and ominous odds, and also in the area of sharing personal spiritual strength with friends.

Another teaching and learning activity which responds to the "what to teach, when to teach, and how to teach" question is then mandatory. It would look like this on a teacher's lesson planning sheet:

Activity/Time	Specifics
Memorization of God's Word. 1-3 minutes at each meal.	Pick a verse to be memorized. Write it down or repeat it orally. Give the children

a time to memorize it.
Review often. Repeat
at mealtimes or bedtimes.
Write the verses and
post them in prominent
places, around the house.

Parent's Role
Pick the verses. Explain them. Say them or write them.
Reinforce with lullabies, songs, audio/ videotapes, and
story books which repeat the themes you've taught. Ask
the children to recite. Review often. Praise your children.

Child's Role
Learn the verses.

Summary

Probably one of the most surprising things about
what is suggested in this chapter is how little time it
actually takes to do a good job, and how many terrific
benefits result from it. Let's review all of the good things
that happen as a result of the wise use of 8-10 minutes a
day:

(1) Development of the habit of praying
      before eating.
(2) Development of the attitude of obedience
      to God, and of faith in God's responsiveness
      to prayer, as well as development of an
      awareness of the parents' concern for spiritual
      growth.

153

(3) Opportunity for practice in prayer, and building confidence in the results of prayer.

(4) Establishing your vital interest in and concern about what is important to your children.

(5) Opening up of channels of communication and trust between you and your children.

(6) Instilling of the value and desirability of taking the time to listen to one another.

(7) Teaching of empathy for one another, and compassion to help one another.

(8) Acknowledgment of the indispensability of the Word of God in our daily lives.

(9) Acquisition of the habit of daily Bible reading.

(10) Growth in spiritual knowledge, insight, and faith in God.

(11) Confidence in witnessing to others.

(12) Possession of peace of mind and strength in adversity, increased responsiveness to others, growth in capacity for triumphant Christian living, and increased usefulness job, to Jesus Christ.

Will all of these spectacular things happen if you are not 100 percent consistent--if you miss a few evenings? Absolutely, yes! There are times when there *are* unavoidable conflicts, such as early games, play practice, parents' meeting, school field trips, and other distractions. There are times when a child or a parent will have an obligation which conflicts with the mealtime or evening prayers, study, or discussion. I can speak from personal experience when I say that missing 100 percent consistency will not be harmful. My obligation as a parent has been to keep priorities identified. As a realistic and practical rule of thumb, I try to keep in mind the idea that our spiritual activities, *at a bare minimum,* should be taking place "more often than not." If it turns out, in your home, that they are taking place "more not, than often," it's time to do some serious self inventory and some careful replanning of priorities.

How Much of Your Time is *This* Worth?

During the aftermath of the Columbine High School massacre in early 1999, something took place that only Christians could understand. *The Denver Post* (May 30, 1999, p. 2G, described it like this:

It was clear that faith was invaluable to many hardest hit by the tragedy. On the afternoon of the shooting, reporters were cleared out . . . before victims' parents were notified, but Red Cross volunteer Lyn Duff, who is Jewish, was stunned by the reaction of the [Christian] families to their loss. "It was like 180 degrees from where everybody else was, " she said. "They were singing; they were praying; they were comforting other parents . . ..They were . . . responding a lot to other people's needs. They were definitely in pain, and you could see the pain in their eyes, but they were very confident of where their kids were. It was like they were a living example of their faith."

Triumph in tragedy.   Triumph for parents. Triumph for their children.   Triumph for the victims. Triumph for the survivors.
Power and courage based on the Word of God.

And all it costs is time . . ..

Chapter Ten

Discipline: Whose Responsibility?

Meet Marilyn: She Has Everything, and She Has Nothing

Marilyn is a woman who has everything. She is beautiful, intelligent, socially aware, and admired--even envied--by women who know her professionally and socially. Her husband is a successful businessman who has provided her with the best of everything. She is a dedicated Christian whose friends seek her counsel, and whose three children, two teenagers--a boy and a girl--and a pre-teenage daughter, are popular and well-mannered at school and in the community.

Yet Marilyn is miserably unhappy, for despite her intelligence, her wit, her social acuity, and her charm, and in spite of the fact that her friends and her real estate clients respect her advice and counsel, in her home she is patronized by her husband and ignored by her children, or worse yet, spoken to condescendingly by her children, as though she is the village idiot. Consequently, Marilyn is unable to direct the behavior of her children. She cannot get them to do household chores. She cannot get them to obey her. Frequently, her children laugh derisively at her directives. Even her youngest child, who is barely twelve years old, refuses to attend church or Sunday school. In short, she is a slave in her own household. She also has become the villain in her family's continuing drama: the silent and subtle struggle between mom and dad for ascendancy in the eyes of the children. Dad, like many other dads, talks down to his wife and makes her look foolish, and even though he is respectful, he is patronizingly respectful, thereby showing his children that their mother is to be treated with the same kind of deference one would grant to a faithful family canine during "Be Kind to Animals Week."

So Marilyn continues in her misery, while her children are raised in a divided house in which Marilyn's husband does not provide support as she attempts to train her children, and, in reality, who exacerbates the situation by overruling Marilyn when she seems to be "too strict," or "too fussy."

Richard and Ava

Richard and Ava have a similar situation, only in reverse. Richard's son, Jonathan, is timid, emotionally immature, and socially behind most children his age. Ever since Jonathan has been a little child, Ava has openly challenged Richard's decisions about Jonathan, often overruling him in front of Jonathan. Jonathan now has it all figured out. Richard is the aggressor, Ava the protector. The situation is so bad that Richard cannot even shout encouragement to Jonathan at the middle school basketball game, because Jonathan immediately interprets Richard's shouts as criticism. Unless drastic changes are made, no further communication between father and son will *ever* occur.

The Joke is on Mom, But it's no Joke

Mom is not ignored in Donna's household. She's just the butt of all the family jokes, and has been the "helpless female" for nineteen years. Two of her children have no confidence in her whatsoever, ignoring her advice and paying no heed to her opinions. They often join in during the "bugging" sessions during which mom is "teased" for her idiosyncrasies and her "cute little" ideas. The other child, newly-exposed to the feminist perspective, silently regards her father and her siblings with contempt for what they are doing to her mother, for whom she has no respect for putting up with the "putting down." Needless to say, Mom's opinion doesn't mean much to her, either.

Jane: She Saw Trouble Ahead, and Took Action

In a fourth home, thanks to the grace of God, a similar situation was averted by Jane. When the children were very small, they discovered that dad's answers to requests were often different from mom's answers, so they began to ask him for certain privileges which would be likely to be denied by mom, and vice versa. On several occasions, dad good-naturedly--but in front of the children--chided mother about her "hyper" attitude toward the kids, suggesting that her concerns were without foundation, emanating, even from an "overprotective mother" attitude. Jane, city-bred and socially-refined, realized that Herb, whose playground had been his family's ranch, really did delight in her seeming "tenderfootedness," and really did chuckle at what to him was a genuinely and excessively overprotective attitude. But Jane didn't ignore the potentially destructive interactions which were occurring in their home. As Herb explained it to me, Jane took him aside one day, after he and the children had enjoyed a good laugh at one of her "tenderfoot" concerns, and said, "Herb, I really don't mind when you tease me about being overprotective; I know you're probably right. I also know why the children ask you for permission most of the time when they want to do something, instead of asking me, and I don't blame them. But Herb, even though we might disagree about some things, we have to stick together and present a united front to the children. You can tease me all you want, but you can't tease me about my decisions in front of the children, because they will learn to lose respect for me, and I don't think I could bear that."

Herb's children are grown up and independent now. I have watched in awe as they have honored their father and their mother, deferring to them not out of obligation, but out of genuine respect. Herb, in response to my question about "landmark incidents" in raising kids, asserted, "I think the day Jane took me aside when the kids were very young, when she pointed out where we were heading with our divided attitudes, was the most significant single incident in our success in raising the children. After that conversation, we often had vigorous disagreements about certain decisions in raising the children, but we never disagreed in front of them. We presented a united front. In fact, we often would joke, after our children had departed following a difference of opinion with us, "United we stand; divided we fall." I can say, without a doubt, Jane's insistence that I treat her with respect, and her desire that we present a united front, was the most significant incident in raising kids in twenty-three years!"

Divide and Conquer

"And if a house is divided against itself," declared the Son of God in Mark3:25, "that *house will not be able to stand."* The fact that the words of Jesus are true has been borne out again and again throughout history. Nations have been torn asunder by civil war. There are families in which divisions are so painful and deep that family members do not even speak to one another. Military experts are well aware of the theme, "divide and conquer"; the strategy has been used in every military theatre in every era of history in every corner of the globe, from local skirmishes to international conflagrations.

Whose Responsibility? The Answer is Obvious

There is truly abundant evidence substantiating the truth of Jesus' teaching that a house divided against itself cannot stand. So then, as with the answers to so many other questions, the answer to this question--"Whose responsibility is discipline?"--is obvious. It is *both* parents' responsibility, and although, as we shall see later, each parent has a unique role, both parents have the responsibility to present a *united front*.

The first condition, therefore, which must be established for constructing a program of effective discipline **must** be this:

Discipline that can't fail must be based on the Word of God. *Both* parents share the responsibility to agree on the essentials of discipline. It follows, then, that:

> *Both parents* have the responsibility to agree on *what* will be taught.

> *Both parents* have the responsibility to agree on *when it* will be taught.

> *Both parents* have the responsibility to agree on *how* it will be taught.

> *Both parents* have the responsibility to agree on *who* will teach it.

What About Single Parent Families?

If there is only one parent, the parent must be consistent--deviating from the program of discipline only when it can be made clear to the child that there is a logical, valid reason for a lack of consistency from one situation to another.

The beginning of this book stated a God-given guarantee that if we train up a child in the way he should go, when he is old he will not depart from it. It seems desirable at this point to state another guarantee--not one based on the positive promise of God Almighty, but one which has evolved from the negative results of the bitter experiences of parents who did not bother to plan their strategy of discipline and who ended up bickering about discipline-related decisions in front of their children. Or, they proved by their lack of consistency that they were "of a divided mind", or unsure, about what they were doing, and their kids picked that up.

The guarantee is simple: *"If both parents do not carry out their responsibility to present a united front in providing discipline--that* is, if they do not agree with one another on "what," "when," "how, "and "who," *they will be virtually guaranteed to fail!* I have little hesitation in asserting this guarantee. I think of Ken, who spends hours talking to me, who loathes his father--the one who always said no--and who tolerates his mother, who let him do almost anything he wanted to do. When the money for college tuition stops, Ken has vowed that his future contact with his parents will stop. He wants nothing to do with either parent. "They lay their trip on me," he complains, "and it's like a contest to see who is the best loved parent. It's like they never talk about being a family, capable of just enjoying one another."

Another Example of "A House Divided"

Such is the case with Rene, who wants to go anywhere but home for the holidays, where she has been used for eighteen years as a pawn in a continuing conflict between her parents. Or Lori, who is totally undisciplined and running wild, since the standards of conduct for her were never established; they varied from parent-to-parent and from day-to-day. Lori has no particular loyalties to either parent, who are now divorced. "Whoever sends the plane ticket," she proclaims, "gets the kid. I can do about whatever I want at either place. Neither of 'em knows what's going on, and even if they did, they wouldn't know what to do about it." It's interesting to note as an aside that Lori inevitably becomes romantically involved with males who are domineering and abusive.

Besides the responsibility of presenting a united front--of agreeing on the program of training--there are other responsibilities which belong to both parents:

(1)   Both parents have an obligation to know and understand what God requires of them.

Obviously, you can't do what God wants you to do if you don't know what he wants you to do. You can't hang in there when the situation is tough if you don't have a knowledge of what to hang on to. You can't persevere and stick to doing what is the right thing to do if you don't know what is the right thing to do.

(2)   It is both parents' responsibility to show
       mutual respect and care for one another.

Children are great imitators. The best way to discipline them to respect their parents is to respect and honor your spouse. This giving of respect and honor, incidentally, is one of the things God requires of married couples (I Corinthians 11). Once again, there's a negative guarantee in operation here. If husbands and wives show respect and honor to one another, *it is probable* that their children will show respect. *It is inevitable*, though, that children will not respect their parents if the model they see is that parents do not respect one another.

There is another very intriguing aspect to giving the respect and care which God demands. It is amazing that there are always practical ramifications connected to God's commandments. For example, one problem which comes up over and over, and which is probably the only problem which still hits me hard emotionally, is the problem of physical abuse. A student limps into my office. It is late afternoon; dusk has already descended. She's been at home all day. She tearfully tries to communicate to me, through swollen and bruised lips, that she missed class because of a beating she received at the fists of her boyfriend. An hour later, after we have mulled over the situation, she informs me with tears in her eyes that, despite my protestations to the contrary, she "probably deserved it." Where did she get the weird idea that she deserved violent physical abuse? Her dad systematically, and with regularity, verbally and physically abused her mother.

Another student, an outstandingly attractive young woman by anyone's standards, tolerates public humiliation, foul language, and abusive treatment from her boyfriend, whose behavior patterns are exactly those of her father toward her mother.

Yet another beautiful young woman, a product of a home in which her parents contemptuously treated one another, almost pathologically pursues relationships in which she and her current romantic interest are abusive to one another.

Over the years I've encountered situations like these, in which young people have tolerated abuse. In some cases I've wondered if some of them have actually *sought* abuse. But over all those years, I have never seen even *one* case in which a young man or young woman, raised in a home in which the parents respected and honored one another--would tolerate an abusive relationship.

The result of the parents' meeting their responsibility to provide discipline through the showing of mutual respect and honor has many ramifications. Not only do children learn to respect their parents. They also learn something equally as fundamental to effective discipline. *They learn to respect themselves.*

We now have two responsibilities which are shared by both parents: knowing what God expects of them, and respecting and honoring one another. Let us look at a third responsibility which is shared by both parents.

(3)   It is both parents' responsibility to provide correction when necessary.

What if Your Child Were Drowning?

A child is in serious trouble, flailing his arms and thrashing in panic, unable to keep from floundering in deep water, gurgling and choking, gasping for help because he's in over his head. His mother stands nearby, wringing her hands, totally alarmed by what is happening. "Wait 'til your father gets home!" she exclaims.

Ridiculous? Of course. If your child is drowning, you don't say, "Wait 'til your father gets home." You plunge in immediately, regardless of how traumatic the situation is, and correct it. It is not the father's exclusive prerogative to extricate the child from a hazardous situation.

It is the responsibility of each parent to minister to the needs of the child. If one parent provided no food for the child, would the other parent watch the child starve, or hope that the offending parent would act more responsibly? If one parent failed to provide clothing or shelter, would the other parent passively watch the child shiver, lapse into hypothermia, and die? If one parent failed to provide medical care for an ailing child, would the other parent stupidly stare at his suffering offspring, wishing that his mate would show more initiative? In the same way, both parents have a responsibility to instill discipline, to provide guidance, and to administer correction. When you "pass the buck," you do much more than that. You bankrupt your whole account, and if you should ever need to draw on any reserves, you'll find that you have no authority--you've passed the buck to your spouse so many times that you have no bucks left.

One of the first principals I ever worked for as an elementary school teacher taught me an invaluable lesson which I passed on to my teachers when I became a principal. This specific principal was especially forbidding. Just to receive "the look" from him was enough to metamorphize a would-be delinquent into a model citizen in mere seconds. But he had one standing rule. No child was ever to be sent to the office for discipline. His theory, which was proven correct even with the toughest students, was that every time a child left the classroom to go to the principal's office, some of the teacher's authority and credibility left with the child. "I'll support any reasonable action you wish to take," he would often say, "but I will not allow you to surrender your effectiveness and authority by sending a child to me for discipline."

I have often thought of his statement as I have supervised student teachers. I would walk through the halls of schools where children were lined up 8-10 deep, awaiting correction from the vice principal for student affairs--whatever that was--while their classmates wreaked continuing and unrestrained havoc in the capitulating teachers' classrooms.

Discipline is both parents' responsibility. In the sense that the provision of discipline is one of the finest expressions of love between a parent and a child, it is as absurd to think of a parent saying, "Wait until your father (or mother) gets home," when correction is needed, as it would be absurd to say, "Wait 'til father (or mother) gets home," when the child asks for a hug.

A Fourth Shared Responsibility

A fourth, and final responsibility which is shared by both parents is this:

(4) It is *both* parents' responsibility to teach whenever possible.

The accounts of Jesus' teachings in the Gospels show how Jesus used events around him to teach God's truths. Someone would point to people giving an offering, and from that situation the lesson of the widow's mites would emerge. The glories of the temple would be extolled, and another lesson would result. From an argument among the disciples on "greatness" would be born a penetrating explication of humility. From a simple act of footwashing the great story of forgiveness and thankfulness was developed. In each case, Jesus, who was intensely aware of his major mission in life, conveyed the love of God to His disciples through capitalizing on the opportunities provided by people, events, and conversations which comprised the setting for His day-to-day activities. We, too, can capitalize on people, events, and conversations in pursuing the effective carrying out of our major responsibility as parents, teaching our children about the love of God. And the job does not require a teacher's certificate or a degree in theology.

We teach whenever we are our children's role model as we respond to difficult situations with a faithful and trusting heart. We teach when we provide time for a friend, or show patience when we're provoked. We teach when we observe love or lack of it in the actions of strangers and then discuss the situations we observe. We teach when we discuss events on the playground, on the athletic field, in the classroom, on television, or in the world or local news.

Two girls in the neighborhood where we once lived were laughing over the plight of one of their classmates, obviously relishing the chagrin which would surely be experienced by their rival when she returned to school after an absence, only to discover that the performance for which she had especially practiced and for which she would be wearing a special costume that day had been rescheduled. Their mothers, who were in the next room, overheard the laughter, and capitalized on the opportunity to discuss feelings, kindness, love, and consideration for others. No mention was made of the fact that it would be kind of the girls to apprise the would-be performer, an admitted "grandstander," of the postponement. Nevertheless, the girls were moved to call the grandstander and tell her about the postponement. No, the girl did not become their bosom buddy. Not only that, she wasn't even "properly" grateful. And when the rescheduled event provided the opportunity, she stole the show. But then again, God didn't tell us that if we taught our kids the right way, "The stones on their paths shall indeed be as the softest marshmallows." He merely told us to *teach* the lessons. The Holy Spirit will provide the major learnings.

Responsibilities: Let's Review Who Does What

Responsibilities: Let's Review Who Does What

At this point, let's review. Four main tasks were identified as the responsibility of *both* parents:

(1)   Both parents have an obligation to know what God requires of them.

(2)   Both parents have the responsibility to show respect and care for one another.

(3)   Both parents have the responsibility to provide correction when necessary.

(4)   Both parents have the responsibility to teach whenever possible.

There are other responsibilities besides those which are the job of both parents. God lays out some concerns which are uniquely the responsibility of the father. And he describes others which are uniquely the responsibility of the mother.

It is very important to be unequivocally aware of the fact that it is God, Himself, who has described the responsibilities and roles for each parent. Only by systematically tossing away a part of the Bible here and a part there is it possible to miss the fact that God has carefully laid out two different sets of responsibilities for each parent, in addition to the responsibilities held in common. And it really doesn't make any difference whether "modernists" like this fact or not. Vitriolic attacks and an avalanche of criticism don't change it. It's totally irrelevant whether they agree with it or accept it. The only thing we as parents need to know, if we want to provide discipline that can't fail, is, "What does God say?" We do not have to *like* what God says. We just have to *do* what God says, regardless of whether our scintillatingly articulate acquaintances in the *avant garde* accept it or not, for, as the Scripture says, ". . . God's words will always prove true and right, no matter who questions them," (Romans 3:4 TLB) and that, ". . . your job is not to decide whether the law is right or wrong, but to obey it" (James 4:11 TLB). What follows then are two different, but overlapping and complementary sets of responsibilities, one for the father, and one for the mother, in providing the conditions for discipline that can't fail.

The Father's Responsibilities

It is the father's responsibility, first and foremost, to be the priest of the household. He must, therefore, accept and carry out, to the maximal extent that God gives him the grace to do so, the role of spiritual *leader of the household*. Therefore, the father must accept the responsibility for the spiritual development of his wife and his children, for as the Scripture tells us in 1 Corinthians 11, *"the wife is responsible to the husband, the husband is responsible to Christ, and Christ is responsible to God."* Now it would be idiotic absurdity to debate *what* the husband is responsible *for* in an attempt to evade the issue that the husband is responsible for spiritual development. "What *could* the Scripture

171

possibly mean?" Does it mean that the husband is responsible for mowing the lawn? That he is responsible for cooking the meals? Paying the bills? Getting everyone off to school and to work on time? Servicing the family car? Keeping big and dangerous neighborhood dogs from molesting the family? Such mental gymnastics would be absolutely inane and ludicrous. The husband has a primary responsibility which cannot be ignored:

The husband and father is responsible for providing the conditions necessary to help the wife and the children grow in faith in Jesus Christ.

To accomplish this end, it follows that the husband must diligently:

(1) Seek first the kingdom of God and His righteousness. The husband must be responsible for his own spiritual growth (Proverbs 20:7).

(2) Pray for his wife and children.

(3) Teach his children and be responsible for his wife's growth in spiritual knowledge (Ephesians 5:21-33).

(4) Bring the children up with the loving discipline the Lord Himself approves, with suggestions and godly advice (Ephesians 6:4).

(5)   Provide an atmosphere of loving kindness,
        not one filled with harshness, bitterness, and
        scolding and nagging (Colossians 3:19-21).

The husband, in pursuing these responsibilities, will benefit from the counsel and suggestions of his wife, who has been provided by God to be his helpmeet, but the husband, with the help of God, should make his own decisions. The father, then, must *require that* his wife and children do those things which will help them grow spiritually; the father must not *request* that they do this.

The Mother's Responsibilities

As indicated, the preceding discussion may rankle many advocates of equality of the sexes, but the situation is not as one-sided as it may seem. Let us turn now to the responsibilities which are unique to the wife. First, it is the primary responsibility of the wife to be the "helpmeet" in the home. That is, the wife is to help the husband. And what is the wife required to help the husband do? Mow the lawn? Wash the car? Advance in rank and salary at work? While it might be argued that any man would most certainly be blessed to have a wife who would help him do these things, and that these things might legitimately be some of the things a wife might be able to do to help her husband, it can more readily be argued that, if the wife is to help the husband, her help must be available in the area which is her husband's primary responsibility. The most earnest effort of the wife, obviously, should not be applied to those areas which are the husband's secondary or tertiary responsibility. The most zealous energies of the wife obviously should not be expended in helping her husband meet his lesser responsibilities. The primary responsibility of the wife, therefore, the area to which her best energies and efforts should be devoted, is to help her husband meet his primary responsibility; namely, that of being the spiritual leader of the home. The wife, therefore, has the responsibility to help her husband be a spiritual leader. To accomplish this end, the wife has the responsibility to submit to her husband's leadership (Colossians 3:18, 1 Corinthians 11:3, Ephesians 5:21-33). If the wife does not submit to her husband's leadership, her husband cannot conceivably, by any stretch of the imagination, be a leader. One cannot, by definition, be a leader, if there is no one following. The woman is indispensable to God's plan for the family, and God painstakingly points out the significant status of the wife and mother, rendering indefensible the conclusion that the woman is of lesser importance than the man, or that the mother is of lesser importance than the father.

Leadership and followership are analogous to the idea of a sequence. Sequence is not possible to attain unless there is a part which is the beginning and a part which follows, each of which is a vital, indispensable, and equally important part of the whole.

According to God's plan, the mother has unique responsibilities:

(1)   To help her husband carry out his role as the spiritual leader of the family (I Peter 3:1-7).

174

(2)   To be responsible for her own spiritual growth.

If the mother carries out these significant responsibilities, the conditions for a program of discipline that can't fail will have been established. And in the tragic or unfortunate eventuality of the loss of the husband and father as a spiritual leader due to separation through death, divorce, or other difficult circumstances, the mother will be unquestionably able to assume the responsibility for the spiritual welfare of her children. Admittedly, her job in these circumstances will be difficult, but no more difficult than the job of a father who does not have the support and assistance of a spiritually motivated wife.

What Are the Children's Unique Responsibilities?

It comes as a surprise to most parents--and to most children too--that God places some heavy demands upon children participating in discipline. Here is a sample of what God says:

> *Children, obey your parents; this is the right thing to do because God has placed them in authority over you. Honor your father and mother (Ephesians 6:1,2) (TLB).*

You children must always obey your fathers and mothers, for that pleases the Lord (Colossians 3:20 TLB).

God also tells children that "*. . . kindness should begin at home, supporting needy parents.   This is something that pleases God very much*" (1 Timothy 5:4) (TLB), and to Timothy God says, "*Never speak sharply to an older man, but plead with him respectfully just as though he were your own father*" (I Timothy 5:1) (TLB). In Proverbs, children are told, "*Hearken to your father who begot you, and do not despise your mother when she is old*" (*Proverbs* 23:22).   God considers the respect and honor of a child for his parents to be of such magnitude that He says, in Exodus 21:15, "*Whoever strikes his father or his mother shall be put to death.*"

Notice, too, that besides placing an obligation upon children, God also provides a beautiful promise:

Honor your father and mother.   This is the first of God's Ten Commandments that ends with a promise. And this is the promise; that if you honor your father and mother, yours will be a long life, full of blessing (Ephesians 6:2,3) (TLB).

From the commands of God, we can infer specific behaviors expected from children. We see that the responsibility of children in a program of Christian discipline is that they are required to:

(1)   Obey their parents.
(2)   Honor their parents.
(3)   Take care of their parents.

176

(4) Speak respectfully to their parents.

(5) Listen carefully to their parents.

But how, many parents ask, can *children* know what they are supposed to do?

That's simple. They know because their father and mother have carried out their shared responsibility to *teach* their children. And the subject matter has been reviewed, reinforced, and revitalized each time the father has pursued his unique responsibility to help his child grow spiritually, and each time the mother has pursued her unique responsibility to help the father provide the conditions for spiritual growth. The whole situation is cyclical. The children help their parents to meet their responsibilities because the parents help the children to meet their responsibilities.

How To Get Your Children to Respect You

The cycle of mutual help in providing mutual growth is a cycle similar to the one described in 2 Peter 1: 1-6. There, Peter tells us that, if we want more of God's kindness and peace, we must get to know Him better; as we get to know Him better, the more we will grow strong spiritually. Similarly, the more parents demand that their children respect them, the more the children will respect their parents; the more they respect their parents, the more the parents can teach them what God expects of them.

177

You'll notice that the sentence above says that parents "demand" that their children respect them. That's not a careless use of the word. One mother recently related to me how she and her husband had been ignoring their fourteen year-old son's sullen behavior because they had been led, along with other parents in their Christian school, to believe that surliness and sullenness were "natural" for teenagers. Well, "natural" it may be. But "acceptable" it is not. It will become natural if we don't nip it in the bud. If you do not demand respect from your child, you're, in effect, subsidizing sinful behavior. It's as simple as that. It's like watering and fertilizing a weed patch.

When we think about whose responsibility it is administer Christian discipline, one conclusion is inescapable: Christian discipline is the responsibility of every member in the family.

Who Else Can Help?

Larry had a problem. And the problem was obviously a very pressing one, because Larry ignored the travelers' advisories dominating the weather forecasts and drove thirty miles down the twisting highway in The Big Thompson Canyon to seek advice. He had called Jim, one of his Christian professors, and asked for his opinion. He had talked to me on the telephone two days before the deadline for his decision. He had sought the counsel of Wally, a good friend in the Fellowship of Christian Athletes. And now it was deadline day, and as Larry put it, "The Lord still hasn't told me what to do." Little matter that Jim and Wally and I had prayed for guidance to help Larry reach a decision, and that we had all concurred in our suggestions to Larry. The puzzling fact, as far as Larry was concerned, was that, "The Lord hasn't told me, in clear terms, what to do. I've listened for His voice, but all I get is the same silence every time I listen."

Sometimes We Miss the Obvious, Because We're Not Looking

The trouble with Larry was not that God was not guiding, or that Larry wasn't listening. God was, indeed, guiding. Larry was listening for an answer from the clouds, which he hoped would be audible in his head. God was providing an answer, in the meantime, through the advice of Larry's friends, who had sought the guidance of the Holy Spirit before offering their opinions to Larry. Too often the handiwork of the Holy Spirit, which comes through the hands of friends in Christ, is not recognized. We overlook the apparent as we seek for the apparition. Our Christian friends constitute one of the most highly significant resources we could ever hope for in helping us in discipline our children. They too are able to provide teaching, role modeling, and companionship for our children.

Steve, for instance, is the epitome of the rugged outdoorsman. He loves to hunt, hike, and fish. He thrives on the scent of sagebrush and lodgepole pine, and the bite of a frosty November morning in the mountains on his face as he silently stalks big game. It's one of the few things he doesn't do with Frank, his best friend, who grew up in the inner city on the plains and whose idea of an outdoor excursion is to light the barbecue in the backyard and move the lawn chair from the shady spot under the trees, and who doesn't know a shotgun shell from a rifle bullet. Frank's son, Frank Jr., having grown up in an environment different from his dad's childhood environment, is an outdoor nut. His biggest anticipated thrill is when he'll turn fourteen, and be able to hunt big game, a thought which, to say the least, is a complete turnoff for Frank, who not only does not know anything about big game, he doesn't *want* to know anything about big game. Frank Jr. has learned that his dad has nothing to say if the conversation is about the outdoor life of the hunter and fisherman. To make matters worse, there hasn't been that much to say between father and son for quite some time. The ingredients are present for cooking up the classic batch of problems. Father and son don't communicate much to begin with. Father and son don't communicate at all on son's all-consuming passion. Father has no interest at all in son's interest, nor does he have any idea or desire to even to try to become interested.

So what are friends for? Enter Steve. All the ingredients are there to cook up a smorgasbord of great experiences between Steve and Frank Jr. And Steve and Frank Jr. build a camaraderie which had been almost irretrievably lost between Frank Senior and Frank Junior. But it's not as big a communication barrier as it seems, because, thank God, Frank Sr. can work through Steve.

Steve has been provided by God as a smooth, clear channel of communication to get to Frank Jr.

Remember the anecdote about the drowning child mentioned at the beginning of this chapter? Wouldn't it be criminally stupid of a father, downstream in a tumultuous current, to refuse to allow his friend upstream, who is the holder of a lifesaver's certificate, to plunge in and save his child, because the father's attitude was one of, "I should be the one to save my son, even if it means going against the current."

Too frequently, blind pride keeps us from using, for the benefit of our children, the qualities of our friends, who may be, in certain instances, better equipped than we are to deal with a given situation.

Use The Resources God Has Provided: Especially Friends

Are you fully using your God-given resources? Look around. If you see a friend who is or could be a role model, tell him or her. Example upon example could be given about how effective it is to utilize the friends or relatives God has given us to help us raise our children. Not all the examples involve male-to-male relationships, of course, but one more vivid example stands out, and in this case, it also happens to be male-to-male.

One of my students at the university, who teaches a high school Bible study group, is extremely knowledgeable about weight training, and has been blessed with a physique which pays tribute to both his proficiency and his hard work in body-building and weight training. He is obviously a role model for young people. To many of them, weight training and body-building are extremely important. Here was a God-given opportunity for me, as a father, to help my teenagers grow spiritually and physically! My student, who valued his abundant expertise in weight training and his depth of knowledge in body-building as gifts of God to be shared with others, was more than willing to graciously take his time to plan a training program and to work with my teenagers. His obvious knowledge, competence, and confidence came through with great force. That gave him, by inferential association, instant and continuing credibility as a trusted Bible class teacher. I shared with him my thought that I was deeply aware that my children saw him as a role model, and he knowingly and willingly became one of my many partners in building a program of discipline that can't fail.

The Role of Grandparents

Any book on the effective utilization of human resources in the Western world, if it included a section on "unexplored potential" or "underutilized resources," would most assuredly include a section on senior citizens. Unlike the cultures of the East, in which reverence for maturity of years is the established and cherished custom, the older generation in the Western world is often tolerated and endured, its potential sagacity and insight ignored by its children.

In later years, they wonder why their own children seem to merely tolerate and endure them, "After all we've done for them." There is no doubt that in some cases, grandparents can create some problems for parents in the area of child-rearing. Consider the following letter to Dear Abby:

DEAR ABBY: I am the mother of an adorable two-year-old I'll call "Karla." Ever since her birth, the relationship between my mother-in-law and me has deteriorated until I can barely tolerate her.

"Gamma" bought Karla's entire layette, furnished her room and has clothed her from diapers to christening dress to snowsuits and swimsuits. Before I can save the money to buy something special for Karla, it is purchased, gift-wrapped and delivered! If I resist, I get the old "What are grandmothers for?" Every weekend Gamma calls and asks if she can baby-sit. When I let her come, she changes Karla's clothes every two hours, combs her hair a different way, and when Gamma leaves she is in near tears because she will miss "her" baby.

When Gamma is around, whatever Karla wants, Karla gets. Naturally, Karla loves having Gamma around. All this makes me feel so inadequate and unneeded. When I complain to my husband, he refuses to "take sides." Next year he will graduate from college. (His mother is paying for his education, too.) He will have a degree, enabling him to relocate anywhere he wants to go. Do I have the right to give him an ultimatum-either we move at least ten hours away from his mother, or I take Karla and move without him?

He is blind to the way his mother manipulates us. She has bought her way into our lives and I am sick of it! Please help me.

-SMOTHERED IN MAINE

DEAR SMOTHERED: Don't issue any ultimatums unless you are prepared to leave your husband. Some firm ground rules must be established concerning the limits of what Gamma may and may not do, but you can't do it alone. This is a family affair that will require professional family counseling. Please get it. All of you! Your marriage depends on it.

Abby's advice is solid; if agreement is reached between husband and wife on what their expectations are, and if their expectations in discipline are shared with the grandparents *before* problems emerge, the grandparents can be of great help in maintaining a program of discipline that can't fail.

If the parents carry out their mutual responsibility to know what God expects of them in providing discipline, and if they carry out their responsibility to agree on the *"what," "where," "how,"* and *"who"* of discipline, it is a very simple matter to explain to grandparents their important role in the plan as they relate to your children. Most grandparent-parent conflicts emanate from the desire of the grandparents to attain importance, stature, or significance in the eyes of their grandchildren, without realizing that it is not necessary to win a "good-guy bad-guy" contest with the parents. If the parents accord to the grandparents the respect and honor God commands, and if they do this in full view of the children, there will be little possibility of a struggle for status.

Grandparent Power: What are the Positives?

Rather than focus on potential negatives, let's look at the benefits.   There are powerful and fruitful contributions to spiritual training that can be made by grandparents. There are lots of ways grandparents can help parents in providing a program of discipline that can't fail.

You will recall that in the section of this chapter under the heading "What Are the Children's Unique Responsibilities?," the first responsibility of children is to obey their parents by following this commandment:

Honor your father and mother (Ephesians 6:2).

You will recall, also, that it is the responsibility of both parents to teach the children their responsibility. Notice that the commandment does *not* say: "Honor your father and mother IF":

(1)   They do not talk too much.
(2)   They refrain from being opinionated.
3)   They do not become too dependent.
(4)   They remember to exercise good personal hygiene, and dress neatly.
(5)   They earn honor and respect by being reasonable, young at heart, and "with it."

No. The commandment says briefly and simply, and with no exclusionary clauses or extenuating circumstances, *"Honor your father and mother."*

Consider the commandment in the light of these familiar expressions, which most of us have heard one or more times:

"What you do speaks louder than what you say."

"Do as I say, not as I do."

"Actions speak louder than words."

"Imitation is the sincerest form of flattery."

Then, consider these "IFS":

IF a child will have a long life, full of blessing,

IF he honors his father and mother; and

IF he must be taught this responsibility; and

IF his parents teach him responsibility; and

186

IF his parents teach best by example, since actions

do, in fact, speak louder than words;

THEN IT LOGICALLY FOLLOWS that you can teach your child his primary responsibility in a program of discipline that can't fail--the responsibility of honoring and respecting his parents--by honoring your own parents. Which means that your children see that you really believe that:

(1)   Parents are prayed for.
(2)   Parents are asked for their opinions.
(3)   Parents are treated with courtesy and respect.
(4)   Parents are written to or telephoned when they are absent.
(5)   Parents are a gift from God.

Deference to and respect for elders is also taught to your children when you obey God's command that, "*You shall rise up before the hoary head, and honor the face of an old man*" (*Leviticus 19:32*).

Remember that, as you pursue a program of discipline for your child, you are sculpting a spiritual man or woman--a spiritual work of beauty who knows and values God's Word, who honors his parents, and who respects his elders and those in authority. A beautiful person, an honor to Jesus Christ, is being created with the help of the Holy Spirit as a result of your obedience to God's commandments.

How the Church Can Help

It may seem out of place to you to find the church mentioned near the end of a list of those who can help with discipline. But the placement in this case is intentional. Not that the role of the church is diminished. But isn't it true that many Christian parents put the church at the head of the list as the agency primarily responsible for the spiritual development of their children? Isn't it true that the church and Sunday school become the *only* place where children hear the Word of God?

Incredibly, some parents who charge the church with this responsibility don't even know who is teaching their children, or *what* is being taught. The church, unfortunately, becomes the convenient "cop out," and parents end up--along with the leaders of many Christian denominations--wondering why, when their children are old enough to be out on their own, the children have no apparent spiritual commitment and no desire at all to attend church or Sunday school. They wonder why there is a strained or uncomfortable atmosphere and embarrassed reluctance among family members when the attempt is made to talk about Jesus. The answer is simple. The parents abdicated their responsibility. Worse yet, maybe the parents didn't even *understand* their responsibility. Often, Jesus *is* not an important part of a young person's life because as the young person was growing up, Jesus *was* not an important part of the child's everyday life. Like the "Sunday best" in shoes, which years ago, were worn with considerable discomfort once a week, and which were never used to travel over rough paths or for everyday living, so is the "Sunday best" faith which is donned once a week, which is worn with considerable discomfort for day-to-day living, and which does not seem to be too helpful for traversing life's rough paths.

But the church need not be a copout. There are so many things the church can do that it would take a whole book on just the role of the church to describe them in full. What follows, therefore, is a very limited sample of what the church can do to provide help in building a program of discipline:

(1)   The church can readily administer the sacraments to families for the strengthening of their faith.

(2)   The church can provide Christian materials for parents and children to help them grow spiritually. For example, it's possible that your pastor suggested the very book which you are now reading.

(3)   The church can provide skilled teachers and spiritually strong counselors for the edification of your family.

(4)   The church can provide youth activities for your children, resulting in spiritually wholesome recreational opportunities and a Christian peer group with whom to associate.

(5)   The church can identify other agencies which can be of help to you in giving your children the best. For example, Campus Life, Campus

Crusade for Christ, and the Fellowship of Christian Athletes are all agencies which can contribute effectively to the building of strong Christians.

The church can also help identify groups with which your child should probably not associate. If you are doing your job at home the way it should be done, there's no need to fear your children's participation in ecumenical groups. I have had the opportunity to work with many groups of different denominations-- including so-called "nondenominational" or "interdenominational" groups, and I have yet to find one young man or woman who has had his or her faith in Jesus damaged because he or she has been guided to associate with other young Christians. The church or denomination in which you are comfortable can provide invaluable guidance to you as a parent in identifying a group of Christian young people whose specific views are compatible with your own, if you are concerned about interdenominational associations.

The church can make many other contributions to your program of discipline that can't fail, including identifying appropriate Scripture verses for your children to learn, identifying interesting Bible stories to be shared, and providing adult fellowship and parent groups for you as you strive to increase your own level of spiritual understanding.

How the Public School Can Help

The school can't help.

That sentence can stand as a paragraph by itself. Decisions in the courts, beginning with the landmark case of Engel v. Vitale in 1962, led to the mistaken notion that the Constitution demanded "separation of church and state" in public education. In fact, most teachers did not know that "separation of church and state" was not included in the Constitution. Therefore, they ended up prohibiting Christian children from expressing their faith in class, writing reports about Jesus, or otherwise giving public testimony to their Christian values.

Even when Christians seek to have balance in the curriculum, they are more often than not met with resistance, and even downright hostility. For example, during my work with school board members, public school administrators, and leaders of professional organizations, I have encountered vigorous resistance when I've asserted that parents, not school officials, should have the final authority to determine what their children should learn. Many officials had the attitude that, even if parents found material to be potentially harmful to their children, that was "tough." Teachers, they said, have the right to ignore parental concerns.

Their attitude can be accurately summarized in the cynical observation of Dr. William V. Mayer, a professor of biology at the University of Colorado in Boulder, who said, about the advocates of equal time for creationism, ". . . they are like Dracula. We thought we drove a silver stake in their heart with the Scopes trial," he mused. He was referring to the 1923 trial in Dayton, Tennessee, in which advocates of the Darwinian doctrine of evolution by natural selection thought they had buried the defenders of the literal truth of the Bible, "but on a suitably dark night, they come alive again."

I have devoted a significant part of my career at the University of Northern Colorado to the "common ground" movement. The movement tried to establish consensus among liberals and conservatives in public education. But I've concluded that consensus is not possible. Secularists and Christians are worlds apart, and some Christians even side with secularists in the schools. Indeed, some of the most vigorous opposition I have faced has come from liberal Christians!

Parents who hope that the schools will enhance the spiritual development of their children are dead wrong! They are incredibly naive. "Religious neutrality" is the goal in public education. For example, in 1999, the *First Amendment Center* in Nashville, Tennessee provided teacher training which advanced the idea that all religions embraced by school constituents deserved "equal time." Christianity was no better than any other religion. Under the goal of "fairness" and "equality", public schools teach an attitude toward Christianity which is exactly the opposite of what Traditionalist Christians teach. We teach that Jesus Christ is *the* Way, *the* Truth, and *the* Life; that He is the *only* Way. Public schools teach the exactly the opposite, and, in fact, regard our beliefs as narrow-minded and bigoted.

Although many fine people teach in the public schools, including many outstanding Christians, their hands are tied; in most districts, they cannot, without fear of reprisal, offer even minimal testimony to their faith.

Ideas Repugnant to Christians

Not only are the hands of Christian school teachers tied, there are many people who teach in the public schools whose ideas are grossly repugnant to Christians. I must confess to considerable past naiveté about this fact, myself. I had an abrupt and shocking awakening on one occasion about how public school teachers' attitudes were foreign from and inimical to the attitudes of Christians. As a matter of fact, I thought that the evidence I was looking at had been accidentally reversed, and that a survey question which I had given, which yielded some shocking answers, had been misunderstood. Here's what happened:

I was teaching a graduate class of about forty adults, all of whom were practicing teachers or administrators working on advanced degrees in education. I had been lecturing on the topic of cultural diversity and on the concomitant point that, while there are a select few values with which most people would agree, there were many other values which would generate vigorous controversy. Since many values would generate controversy, I contended, the logical conclusion which had to be reached about the teaching of values in the public schools, was that teachers had no right to impose their personal values on a captive audience of young children. This would be especially true, I asserted, in teaching at the elementary level. I was thinking about the "anything goes" mentality of my college students in the early seventies, and how the only way I could counsel a lot of them to moderate their sexual promiscuity and forego their affinity for head trips

193

on dope was through appealing to pragmatic practical reasons, rather than to any moral code.

I wanted to point something out to my graduate students. I hoped to show them that the values of what was, in the seventies, the "hippie culture" would be repugnant to them, and that they as parents and experienced educators would not want those values imposed on young children. To accomplish this, I wanted to demonstrate to the class how their values on sex, for one example, were representative of traditional values, and how only a very small minority of them might espouse more liberal values, and would not want these liberal values imposed on young children. So I asked the class this question:

> "How many of you believe in and advocate unrestricted sex between and among consenting adults, without reference to sexual preference or marital status?"

Thirty-eight hands were raised! Two students did not raise their hands. Thinking that my question had been misunderstood, I said,

> "Let me rephrase the question. How many of you believe that it is okay to have sex with anybody you like, whether you are married or not?"

Again, thirty-eight hands shot up, this time with much less hesitation. I was stunned. The two students who did not raise their hands--one male and one female--were a Baptist minister and a Roman Catholic nun.

I have not been at a loss for words on too many occasions in the college classroom, but I was momentarily speechless. The point had certainly been well made, but not as I had intended. It had been well made for me. And for the minister and the nun. And even though many students protested that they did not mean that *they* would be sexually "free," they would certainly not dream of imposing "puritanistic" and "Victorian" values on others. I had to beat a hasty retreat and seize upon an even more flagrant example of value differences, citing child pornography as an area in which my students, as educators, would draw the line. They would not tolerate the promulgation of gross sexual perversity in the public schools. Therefore, the line had to be drawn at both outer limits of values education. Only by using an extreme example was I able to show them that, in public school, they could not inculcate sectarian values at one extreme, or advocate the values of unbridled permissiveness at the other extreme.

Why I Don't Want Religious Values Taught in Public Schools

Since that first shocking awakening--and the incident took place over twenty years ago--I have become more convinced than ever, as I have lectured to teachers across the country, that the public schools cannot and should not teach sectarian religious values. I base my conviction on these experiences: I have heard everything from the untenable hypothesis that Jesus Christ was a mythological character who never lived, to the assertion that God is an all-encompassing nucleus into which all human atoms will be absorbed in the "resurrection" of the body. It has also been suggested to me, in all seriousness by people who identify themselves as Christians but who wish to advocate freedom of sexual preference, that the Apostle Paul was a homosexual, who found prison to be much less traumatic than the Scripture indicates; that God is a woman; and that sexual sin can occur only when married people commit adultery.

During the late nineties, educators who were apologists for the President of the United States asserted that "sexual relations" could be defined in a way that would allow people to expose their private parts for stimulation by others, and claim that, "in a legal sense", their activities were not wrong. I have also heard, in the public schools, that God is unable to keep evil from our lives; that Satan does not exist; that hell is the product of the warped minds of medieval sadomasochists, and that faith in Jesus Christ as the only hope of salvation is the most repulsive of hate-inspired discriminatory doctrines.

Blind Guides End Up in the Ditch

Would you look for assistance in building a strong faith in the heart of your child to an agency which, according to the laws of the land, has to hire people who believe any of the above ideas; or who assert that most of the Bible is fiction, that the writings of Thoreau, Emerson, or Eric Hoffer are just as inspired as the writings of the prophets, the evangelists, and the apostles; and who place their hope of being acceptable to God--if they even acknowledge that there is such a thing as God--in "being sincere" about what you believe? Would you want your kids taught by a teacher who believes that the worst kind of faith is the kind that says that there is only one right way to get to heaven, and that anybody who believes that their way is the only right way is an intolerant, ignorant, and misinformed bigot who, at the very least, should be pitied, and who, for "their own good", should be re-educated?

I am speaking from hard experience when I report to you that there are more weird notions in the classrooms of the public schools, about what it means to be "spiritual" than there are cereals on the shelf at the supermarket. I also know, through repeated experience, that the only notion that is dismissed out of hand as being detrimental to children is Traditionalist Christian spirituality. And I can't begin to tell you how powerful even a raising of an eyebrow, or a smirk, a shrug of the shoulders, or some other condescending gesture can be in affecting your child, if it comes from a coach, a favorite teacher, or some other respected authority figure.

Would you knowingly expose your child to hepatitis over a period of a year or more, if you received free food prepared by professional nutritionists, some of whom might be contagious? And spiritual illness is much more serious than any physical malady! If there is one conclusion I can assert without equivocation, after more than three decades in public education, and after working with literally thousands of teachers, school board

197

members, and other officials connected with public education, it is this conclusion:

The public schools cannot, and should not, have any responsibility to provide the kind of discipline which is discipline that can't fail.

Parents have no right to expect that the public school will provide Christian discipline--training in faith in Jesus Christ. On the contrary, parents would be extremely foolish to desire that the public schools perform this function. Worse yet, parents would be guilty of the worst kind of compromise of beliefs to demand that the schools provide time for "prayer" which is nonsectarian, or for other quasi-religious acts which are all "show" and no substance.

So What Rights Do Christian Parents Have, If They Can't Expect Solid Spiritual Education?

The public school establishment has fought tooth and nail against parents' rights. School officials' attitude is one of "we-know-better-than-you-do-what's-good-for-your-child,"and I am making this observation from personal experience as an advocate for Christian parents' rights before audiences such as the National School Boards Association, the American Association of School Administrators, and other such professional groups. It is complicated, and in some cases, almost impossible, for parents to avoid having their child exposed to content or methods that they perceive to be harmful. In many cases, professional educators believe, simply, that parents really do not know what is best for their own children, and that, in fact, what parents want is not a valid consideration.

But that does not mean parents are totally without rights. For example, they have the right to insist that the public schools maintain an atmosphere of order in which their children can learn without fear of physical or emotional threat. But they should expect that they may have to take school officials to court to secure that right. They also have the right to expect that there will be no imposition of sectarian or quasi-religious teachings, but again, they may have to go to court and argue their case before unsympathetic judges.

You should be aware that, even though parents have the right to demand that religious values not be imposed on their children, that there will be teachings of the public schools which reflect non-sectarian values, and, hence, non-Christian values. The fact that your children will be exposed to overtly unchristian values will have to be both expected and also tolerated. Just as "no man can serve two masters, God and mammon," no school can effectively place two masters on an equal status. Secular humanism and Christianity cannot co-exist with equal status.

Other Parental Rights

Parents also have the right, in many districts, to exercise "choice" by placing their child in a particular school within their district, and they should not hesitate to demand this right. They also have the right of reasonable access to teachers for conferences, consultation,

199

and information about their child, and this right, too, should be liberally exercised.

Despite the availability of parental rights in securing a public school education for their children, and despite the fact that the public schools are ostensibly "neutral" with respect to spiritual training, parents should be aware of several facts. Not only can the public schools not help, the public schools may, in reality, constitute a dangerous threat to a child's development as a devoted follower of Jesus Christ. Even something as seemingly harmless as placing a Nativity Scene on a bulletin board along with a Hanukkah menorrah and Rudolph the Red Nosed Reindeer sends messages: all of the parts of the bulletin board are a part of Christmas, and/or one religious observance is just as valid as another. All the more reason, then, to remember that in a program of discipline that can't fail, the responsibility for providing discipline is first and foremost a shared responsibility of committed Christians. People and agencies which do not focus on commitment to Christ simply cannot be counted upon, even institutions as benign as 4H, the Boy Scouts, Girl Scouts, and so on.

You can tell that what I'm advocating is nothing short of total brainwashing. Even though the activities I've described take only a few minutes, they should be backed up by a total campaign to structure your child's environment. Positive influences should be maximized: Christian books, wholesome juvenile magazines, constructive CDs, videos, movies, and other forms of entertainment should be available. Limits on clothing styles, peer associations (mentioned elsewhere), and various activities should be very clear to you, so you're not groping for a response to any behavior that makes you uncomfortable, and so that you don't end up allowing something that you know, in your heart, isn't good for your child, even though you "can't put your finger on it." Remember that you are in a battle for your child's life!

What You *Have to* Remember: A Review

It seems fitting to end this chapter with one more illustration: Eleven-year-old Josh English, of Greeley, Colorado, was diagnosed with multiple malignant brain tumors in 1997, just six months after his father was killed in a construction accident. On May 27, 1999, the *Greeley Tribune* quoted Josh in a front-page story. His testimony powerfully illustrates what this book is about:

> *"'My mom and Jesus gave me hope,' Josh said."*

Discipline that can't fail is the kind that will prevail even into adult life, and even through hard times. Here are the important facts to remember to achieve it:

(1)   Both parents have a shared responsibility for discipline.
(2)   The father has a unique responsibility and role.
(3)   The mother has a unique responsibility and role.
(4)   The children have a unique responsibility.
(5)   Friends have a useful role.
(6)   Grandparents have a useful role.
(7)   The church has a unique responsibility and role.
(8)   The public school has no responsibility.

Chapter Eleven

How to Handle Undesirable Behavior

Don't Start Here!

There's an interesting characteristic parents share in common. It's the desire to enforce discipline in the most convenient, comfortable, and undemanding way. For this reason, many readers who pick up this book and who peruse the Table of Contents or flip through the pages will probably start reading the book with this chapter. If you're one of these readers, who share with me the desire to get the problem identified, get the problem handled, and get the problem over with, I make the following plea: Don't start with this chapter.

Unless the program of discipline described in the preceding chapters is carefully followed, the procedures described in this chapter won't be satisfactory. On the other hand, if you've followed the program of discipline outlined in this book, the procedures in this chapter will work quite readily. It would not be fair to you, or to me, for that matter, for you to attempt to launch the ship, so to speak, without taking every step possible to make sure that she is seaworthy, particularly when the ship is likely to be buffeted by seas which may be gale-driven, relentlessly challenging, and ominously powerful.

Undesirable Behavior and What to do About It

Several years ago, a particularly heart-rending tragedy rocked a small community in the West. Three young high schoolers, all outstanding athletes, students, and citizens, in a period of temporary stupidity, decided to steal some beer from a delivery truck which was parked behind a liquor store. Coincidentally, the police happened to be on a routine patrol of the area and they noticed the boys acting suspiciously around the truck. Each boy was found to have pilfered a six-pack of beer from the open truck, and the police placed the boys under arrest and took them downtown to the police station. The boys' parents were called and two sets of parents came down to the station to take their sons home. The third boy, however, was allowed to go home on his own, on the promise that he would return the next day with his parents, who could not be reached because they were out of town for the day. There was no hesitation on the part of the police in releasing the boy on his promise. His father was, after all, a prominent citizen in the community, and the boy was known in the community as an outstanding young man. In the minds of the police, perhaps, the purloining of some beer was merely a minor incident of prank-playing-- a high school adventure which would be straightened out with a few words of admonishment from the parents.

Later that evening, the boy's mother and father returned home. They were puzzled by the fact that their son was not at home, but were confident that he would soon show up. After several hours and several phone calls to their son's friends, and after finding out about the pilfering incident, the father became anxious about his son's whereabouts. He called the police for help in locating him, assuming that perhaps he was postponing a confrontation with his father, whom he idolized, and that he was avoiding returning home until after his parents had gone to bed. It was not until dawn that the police located the boy. He was in a little-used vacant garage at the rear of his dad's lot. He had hanged himself!

An investigation into the tragic suicide of the young man revealed that he could not face his parents after having stolen the six-pack of beer. They had had such high expectations of him and they had extolled his virtues so often, that he could not bear to disappoint them. He could not face the hurt which he was sure would be written on their faces. He had failed. So he hung himself.

The tragedy made a deep impression on me. I suffered for the boy's parents, who, like parents everywhere who love their children, would have forgiven their child any transgression, and who would never have voluntarily or knowingly imposed an unbearable expectation of perfection upon their child.

How Do We Set Standards That Aren't Impossible?

How can we teach our children to adhere to the commandments of Christ, and yet teach them, at the same time, to accept and live with their inevitable inadequacies, shortcomings, and personal failures? How can we teach them self-acceptance, and even what is more important, that even though their parents, and God Himself, expect the absolute best of them, their parents will, by the forgiving grace of God, accept the worst of them when they fail--even miserably?

The first thing to teach children, to avert the kind of tragedy described, is to teach them that nobody is perfect, and to fill their hearts with the knowledge of how God handles the fact of our imperfection. Once again, the Scriptures come to our rescue as we attempt what seems like an impossible task to teach our children that God demands that we be perfect but that, through the saving sacrifice of Jesus Christ, He accepts us when we are imperfect.

The story of the Prodigal Son, in Luke 15, is an excellent starting point in explaining this paradox to young children, emphasizing that while the Prodigal Son was *"yet a great way off,"* his father *"saw him, and had compassion, and ran, and fell on his neck, and kissed him."* It is important to emphasize to children at least two of the many significant truths in the parable:

(1)   That the prodigal son was guilty of every conceivable thing which would alienate his father, and

(2)   that, as Jesus says, "when he was yet a great way off," his father "ran to him, threw his arms around him, and kissed him."

In simple terms,
The son had not yet even asked for forgiveness.
The son had not yet made any amends.
The son had not even made himself acceptable in
any way.

Yet his father, because of his great love, *ran* to him,
embraced him, and kissed him! There were no strings
attached. The father was waiting for his son. The only
thing the son did was to turn toward his father, probably
hesitatingly and with great trepidation, with the intent to
seek his father's forgiveness.

First, we must build a foundation of the concept of
the grace of God with repeated retellings of the story of the
Prodigal Son. We must explain the concept of the grace of
God and the spiritual struggles of the Christian. We can
further develop the idea with numerous other Scriptures,
such as the stirring account of the tremendous battle
waged against sin by the Apostle Paul. We can teach our
children what Paul wrote, in Romans 7:15-25 (TLB):

> *I don't understand myself at all, for I really want to
> do what is right, but I can't. I do what I don't want
> to--what I hate.*

> *I know perfectly well that what I am doing is
> wrong, and my bad conscience proves that I agree
> with these laws I am breaking.*

> *But I can't help myself ... it seems to be a fact of life
> that when I want to do what is right, I inevitably do
> what is wrong....*

Oh, what a terrible predicament I'm in! Who will free me from my slavery to this deadly lower nature? Thank God! It has been done by Jesus Christ our Lord. He has set me free.

The Most Important Thing to Remember

The first and most fundamental principle in handling undesirable behavior is to remember that our main goal as parents is to develop in our children faith in Jesus Christ as their Savior. We must teach them that, if they fail, God accepts them through the atonement of Jesus Christ, and that, if God accepts them through Jesus Christ despite their failures to live up to His expectations, we will do no less when they fail to live up to our expectations.

Discipline: What Does it *Really* Mean?

One of the interesting lessons in "How to Teach Vocabulary" to beginning teachers is that, in English, there are no such things as perfect synonyms. That is, no two words mean *exactly* the same thing. Each word, beginning teachers are told, conveys a slightly different nuance. For example, there are different shades of meaning found in the words "smell," "odor," "stink," "aroma," scent,""fragrance," and "bouquet." All of these words deal with the olfactory sense, but they all certainly do not convey the same meaning.

Even more subtle are the shades of meaning conveyed by the synonyms used to get across the ideas embodied in the word "discipline." Consider, for a moment, the shades of difference in meaning between and among the words

punishment
retribution
chastening
correction
guidance
training.

When you picked this book up, the title might have evoked thoughts like, "Oh, boy, now I'm going to find out what kinds of punishments are finally going to work." You might have looked eagerly for an outline of the kinds of negative pressures that would be advocated as methods of "straightening kids out." But the word closest to the meaning of the word "discipline" in this book is the word "training."

"Training," is used as it is found in the verse on which the major premise of this book is based; namely, "Train up"--discipline--"your child in the way he should go, and when he is old he will not depart from it."

Therefore, as Christian parents, we must keep our major purpose in mind when we are confronted with undesirable behaviors. We must bear in mind that undesirable behaviors detract from our main goal: teaching children to follow Jesus Christ. In view of the major goal, then, the most appropriate words to use in handling undesirable behaviors are:

> *training*
> *guiding*
> *correcting-chastening.*

So, Should I Punish My Child for Misbehavior?

Nowhere in this book, to this point, and that covers over two hundred pages of discussion, has the term "discipline" been used in a retributive sense. That is, it has not been used in the sense of punishment, or paying somebody back, for transgressions. *Discipline that can't fail is first, foremost, and only, TRAINING of a child to walk in the footsteps of Jesus Christ, and to follow Jesus Christ as Savior.* It is desirable and necessary, in view of this fact, that wrong behaviors be followed by:

(1)   Correction by the parent:

Which is always a pointing out the right way as compared to the wrong way. Which involves the showing of disapproval, and which *may or may not* involve the application of physical reinforcement or emphasis.

(2)   Another chance for the child:

Training involves repetition. The child should be given opportunities to correct his behavior.

Most certainly, the Scripture states, in *Proverbs 13:24*, *"He who spares the rod hates his son, but he who loves him is diligent to discipline him,"* and in *Proverbs 29:15*, *"The rod and reproof give wisdom, but a child left to himself brings shame to his mother."* But insofar as we "follow after," as Paul says, and seek to be like God, we may also emulate God's methods and His purpose when He reacted to many who sinned by being patient with them. In reacting to the transgressions of those who are responsible to us, we can choose patience, as God did, for the purpose described in Romans 2:4 (TLB):

> *Don't you realize how patient He is being with you? Or don't you care? Can't you see that He has been waiting all this time without punishing you, to give you time to turn from your sin? His kindness is meant to lead you to repentance.*

Just as God does not indiscriminately inflict suffering upon us in each instance in which we fail to *"be perfect, even as our Father which is in heaven is perfect,"* in the same way no judicious and loving parent would advocate the indiscriminate use of the rod of physical punishment in every instance in which a child transgresses.

Neither would a judicious parent advocate that the Scripture should be ignored, and that physical correction is never appropriate.

What, then, is appropriate? Three examples might help.

Arthur is the father of a two-year-old daughter. He teaches his daughter diligently, and he is going to great lengths to instill the love of Christ in her heart. When his daughter disobeys, Arthur corrects her. When he feels that her disobedience, if repeated, would cause her to suffer measurable harm, such as, let's say, a cut finger, burned skin, or more serious danger, he emphasizes his lesson with physical reinforcement which his daughter will associate with the undesirable behavior, and therefore avoid. "I never spank Becky without telling her why I'm spanking her," Arthur says, "And after I spank Becky, I always tell her, 'Daddy and Mommy love you very much,' and then give her a big hug. I think it's extremely important for her to know that physical correction doesn't mean rejection; that it's an expression of our love for her."

Marty, who is the director of a Christian School as well as a successful parent, offers yet another perspective on the use of the rod.

Marty states that, when physical correction is necessary, a literal rod is always used, because the rod of correction should not be confused with "the hand of fellowship." And although Marty believes in the use of a literal rod, even with *teenagers* who "act like immature children" and who are unresponsive to attempts at reasoning, Marty frequently chooses not to use the rod. Instead, he provides correction through verbal persuasion or reprimand.

Doug and Marie, successful parents whose children are responsive and considerate followers of Jesus, have not spanked their children with the rod or anything else, including the hand, since their children were preschoolers. Their children, now teenagers, amusedly reminisce about how just the mere possibility of a spanking was a deterrent to disobedience, and how the threat of the rod added to the persuasive appeal of their parents' directives for appropriate behavior.

How do the experiences of the parents in these three examples provide insight regarding what is appropriate concerning the "rod" of correction? Some readily defensible conclusions seem apparent:

In the training of children, the rod should not be "spared" in the sense that "sparing" the rod means not using it at all. But if careful training in all facets of spiritual growth is diligently undertaken, then the rod will need to be used only "sparingly," in the sense that its use will be required only rarely. The rod, then, is not *spared*, but it's used *sparingly,* which are two totally different concepts.

To Spank or Not to Spank

In our own home, in those instances in which giving children a reason in support of a certain behavior, or giving them a reason as a deterrent to certain behavior would have been wasted on a mind too immature to understand, physical correction was used. In other words, if logic, or explanations, or reasoning with children would not have resulted in a change of harmful behavior, we used a method which would elicit the desired response.

For example, there were cases in which the denying of privileges as a method of correction would have been inappropriate. A very young child might not understand the connection between a transgression and a deprivation of a privilege. At these times, physical correction was timely. It was also vividly recollected and appropriate. As the children matured, they were able to realize and to foresee that certain undesirable behaviors would lead to certain consequences. At that point the *desirability* of using a literal rod diminished. The *frequency of use* of a literal rod also diminished. When we felt that our children had the mental ability and the maturity to understand, we believed that the "rod" of words of correction was more desirable than physical correction. If the behavior persisted, we applied the rod of deprivation of privileges. But when the children did not have the ability to understand the rod of words of reproof or the rod of deprivation of privilege, we used the rod of physical pain.

A rough analogy would be the training of a pup which is inclined to chase cars. The cars can kill. To avoid the tragedy of death to the pup, it might be necessary to apply correction which is painful to the pup, or to physically restrain the pup. Either action would be accompanied by words. Later, as the dog matures under careful training, it might be necessary to apply words only, such as a sharp "NO!" whenever a car approaches. It would not work to say, "I can't bring myself to apply physical pain or physical restraints to a little pup. Instead, I'll spare the rod and explain logically and rationally to the pup the potential ramifications of its undesirable behavior."

The main point to be remembered is that, for every undesirable action on the child's part, there must be a corrective action on the parents' part. To put it succinctly:

Correction, guidance, and training are a part of discipline.
Correction is a way of providing guidance.
Guidance is a way of providing training.
Training is a way of pointing the way to eternal life.

Some Practical Ideas

Arthur, Marty, and Doug each followed some very practical and useful ideas in administering a literal rod of correction to childrenfor the purpose of training them in the "way they should go."

What follows is a list of suggestions drawn from other Christian parents which have worked especially well. The suggestions help provide the kind of environment and atmosphere in instilling the love of Jesus has been made less difficult.

(1) Each child should be treated differently.

No two people are alike, and no two people should be treated in the same way. First, consider this fact on a logical basis. If you have two children, they cannot possibly perceive the world in the same way, since one of them has an older sibling, and the other one does not. Conversely, one of them has a younger sibling, and the other one does not. It may sound foolish, but if you have three children, only one of the three can be the middle child. Other differences are obvious, too. It would be ridiculous to reprimand one child if he did not acquire molars as rapidly as another child, just as it would be ridiculous to reprimand a child who is not as tall as his brother or sister, if he could not reach up to the same heights as his sibling. Jesus also indicated on several occasions that God the Father recognizes our individual differences. Note the Parable of the Talents and the Parable of the Prodigal Son. Without exception, successful parents and teachers cite the recognition of individual differences as one important factor in leading to wise decisions in providing effective discipline. The correction should fit the child.

> (2)   Let your children know what behaviors you expect, and why you expect them.

This principle should be easily recognized, but it is amazing how many children fail to meet their parents' expectations because they do not know what those expectations are. If what you expect is clearly spelled out ahead of time, it will benefit both you and your child. You will not have to make spur-of-the-moment decisions on whether something is allowable or not, and your child will not violate your expectations through ignorance. Know, ahead of time, what you will allow and what you won't allow. Then it will be highly unlikely that you'll make a wrong decision. Even if you're "ambushed" in the middle of   leaving the house or hastening to work or rushing to an appointment or to some other engagement for which you are late, you'll respond wisely. You won't make a hasty and poor decision. The pressure of your child's pleas or the press of time won't affect you.

(3)   Decide *ahead of time*---and tell your children--what the range of consequences will be if they disobey you.

This principle is especially important, because, being human, we are inclined to act rashly or to overreact in anger when we are pushed. Later, when we've cooled down, we often regret our actions and words. Only on audiotape and videotape can actions and words be erased.

If we know what we will do if our children disobey, and if they know what to expect, we will not be as likely to say or do anything we wish later we could erase.

It is also important to include, in the list of consequences, the option of *no* consequence. Stay flexible. Flexibility is extremely valuable. I have told my teacher education students, many times, not to tie their hands by tying a specific consequence to a specific violation. After all, many variables should influence what consquence we use. For example, whether a child realizes what he's done, whether he is remorseful, which of your children violated your expectations, which consequence is most likely to provide the best correction--all these variables can help you make an effective and wise decision.

(4)   Be willing to ask your child for forgiveness when you are wrong.

Diane and Denise, mother and daughter, have a relationship of mutual respect which is inspiring to observe. Diane believes that the development of the respect had its roots in a situation in which she inappropriately spanked Denise for tearing up a bed of tulips which a long-awaited spring had slowly coaxed through the last of a lingering winter's snow. When a neighbor commented, a day later, on how creative and artistic she thought it was that Denise had picked the unfolding tulips to make a bouquet for her snow castle, Diane realized that she had acted hastily and unreasonably, and that the only thing she could do was to apologize to five-year-old Denise and try to make her understand that she had acted inappropriately in spanking her. Just retelling of the incident brought tears of embarrassment to Diane's eyes, but she told me that she approached Denise hesitantly and said, "Denise, I was wrong yesterday when I spanked you for picking the tulips, and I'm very sorry. Will you please forgive me? Denise threw her arms around me, hugged me, and said, 'It's okay mommy. Parents can make mistakes, too, you know,'" Diane recalled. "Since that time, I've made other mistakes, because it's my tendency to overreact and then want to moderate what I've said or done, but Denise has never failed to accept my apologies. I think that my willingness to humble myself when I've been wrong has been a large contributor to our mutually respectful relationship."

I know parents who have complained with bitterness that their children *never* apologized for inappropriate behavior the whole time the children were living at home. These same parents, in response to my questioning, have realized, with some amazement and chagrin, that they themselves had never apologized to their children for their own inappropriate behavior toward their children. Most have used the excuse that an apology would have made them appear weak or foolish in the eyes of their children. But just the opposite is true. Only the weak cannot bear to apologize. It takes a very strong person to ask for forgiveness.

> (5) Provide children with responsibility--with the opportunity to make a positive contribution to the family.

"Never mind. I'll do it myself." These words, exclaimed in exasperation, often evolve from what is readily apparent--that it's often easier and less frustrating to do a job ourselves than to delegate the responsibility, describe what has to be done, evaluate what has been done, and then, too frequently, do the job over the way it should have been done in the first place. Imagine, though, a situation in which *you* are the person at whom the expression of disappointed impatience is directed. Wouldn't you feel inadequate? Incompetent? Useless? Wouldn't your self-respect suffer?

Many parents complain because their children, they say, "do not *see anything* that needs doing around the home." "They expect to be waited on hand and foot." "They seem to take no pride in doing anything useful." But these parents have nothing to complain about. They have *trained their children,* from a very tender age, to do just exactly what the children are doing as pre-teens or teenagers, because the parents have failed to provide their children with responsibilities which would help them grow. *Children become responsible by meeting responsibilities.* Would anyone be so stupid as to hypothesize the reason why his child could not swim, if he had never taken the child into the water? "They don't know what work is!" is the frustrated exclamation of a mother I know, whose teenagers leave their dirty dishes on the table, their school books all over the apartment, their soiled clothing on the floor, their beds unmade, and their junk food wrappers wherever they happened to have been snacking last. Of course, the mother is exactly right. They don't know what work is. Who picked up their toys when they were little children? Mother. Who allowed them to leave their personal possessions strewn randomly all over the apartment? Mother. Who made their beds, even when they were old enough to attempt the task? Mother. Who set the table before the meal, and who picked up the dirty dishes after the meal? Mother. And who sat in silence and failed to notice that his wife had been reduced to the role of serf in a teenagers' kingdom? Father. "Train up a child in the way he should go. . .. " It's ironic. Who trained the children to be ignorant of what work is, and blind to what would easily be seen by any considerate person? Mother and father.

Responsibility Begins at an Early Age

Even very young children can be given responsibility consistent with their ability. What normal child cannot put spoons on the table without breaking them? Even many disabled children can do that. What normal child cannot put his toys in order when he is finished playing with them? One of the biggest favors you can ever do for your child is to place demands upon him.

Perhaps the most responsible, mature, dependable, and self- confident young people I ever met were two young brothers, a seventh-grader and an eighth-grader, who were my pupils in a rural school in Minnesota. They were the hardest workers in the class, could be counted upon to do their best at all times, and they could be trusted to act responsibly even when the teacher was not supervising them. I was so intrigued by the maturity, dependability, and leadership ability of these young brothers that I determined to discover the secret of their parents' success. So I accepted with eagerness an invitation to supper one evening. When I arrived, the father, who was a market gardener, greeted me, explaining that his sons were finishing up with "chores." He matter-of-factly elaborated that they had had a "reasonably" good day, in that he and his sons had planted three thousand onion sets after his sons had arrived home from school. But then again, the boys could handle the task with facility, he explained, because, after all, they had been helping with planting and harvesting after school for several hours each day ever since they were five years old! The whole time the father and I sat and conversed, the man's daughter, age nine, helped her mother set the table and prepare the food, and after the meal, the boys and their sister cleared the table and did the dishes while the parents and I visited. I never got around to asking the parents their secret of success in developing self-confident

228

and responsible children. I didn't need to. Their secret was obvious.

Keep in Mind a Few "Do-Nots."

The five things parents can do, discussed on the preceding pages, take considerably more planning than the few "do-nots" which follow, but the "do-nots" are no less important. The first "do-not" is one which addresses a concern which has probably bothered most parents at one time or another:

1. **Do not** *worry about being too strict.*

If you begin to compare what you are requiring of your children with what other parents are requiring of their children, sooner or later you are going to start worrying about whether you are being too strict. Don't worry about it. You are playing by a different set of rules-- literally--than other parents are. Your goals are different. Your methods are different. Your outcome and results will be different. The source of your authority is different.

Of all the conversations I have had with parents, the overwhelming number are sorry that they were too lenient with their children--too undemanding. Their "should haves" greatly exceeded their "dids." But I have never yet met a parent who said that he was too strict. I am reminded of one parent who remembers with amusement when, as a teenager, she pleaded with her parents, using the well-worn argument, "Everybody's

221

doing it," and was brought up short with the response, "No, everybody's not doing it, because *you're not!*" What the rest of the kids are doing, and what the rest of the kids' parents are doing is totally irrelevant to what you decide to do. Your source of authority is the Word of God, not the word of the neighborhood.

Know what your goal is. Know what your expectations are. Plan your strategy. Then don't worry about being too strict, because you can have the confidence that you are probably the only parents who have embarked upon the journey of child-rearing with a roadmap in hand, so it would be foolish to compare yourself with other parents who do not know where they are going, how they will get there, or what their strategy is.

(2) **Do not** *use sarcasm or embarrassment in an attempt to provide correction. Use praise to provide direction.*

Remember that your purpose is to build character, not to destroy it. Your goal is to develop a positive self-concept, not a negative one. Your intent is to instill pride of achievement, not to create shame in failure. It is often tempting to attain catharsis for ourselves and make ourselves feel better by launching forth with a stinging diatribe at those who disappoint us, but this is a temptation which, with the help of God, we must overcome, because it is potentially so terribly destructive. James, in the third chapter of his epistle, speaks of the destructive power of the uncontrolled tongue, warning his readers, *"Don't be too eager to tell others their faults, for we all make many mistakes,"* and that, *"The tongue is a small thing, but what enormous damage it can do. A great forest can be set on fire by one tiny spark"* (*James 3:1,5*). (*TLB*) Sarcasm, embarrassment, ridicule, and humiliation are disabling. Praise is enabling.

(3) **Do not** *stifle assertiveness.*

When Moses was called upon by God to lead the children of Israel out of Egypt, he demurred, asserting instead his own ideas of what he should be doing.

When God apprised Abraham of his intent to destroy Sodom and Gomorra, Abraham had the temerity to suggest that perhaps a different course of action could be followed!

In each, case, God Almighty showed great patience, allowing both Moses and Abraham to express themselves. Abraham, especially, showed great respect and deference to God: nevertheless, what Abraham was asserting was basically an alternative point of view--a challenge, in essence, to God's point of view. And God allowed the challenge.

Why We Should Allow Our Children to Question Our Decisions

As our children approach young adulthood and acquire increasing ability to think independently, to evaluate critically, and to act responsibly--and they most assuredly will develop these characteristics if we provide discipline according to the commandments of God--it is to

223

be expected that they will begin to question and challenge the appropriateness of our decisions. Do not stifle their questioning or their assertiveness, for a variety of reasons:

a. The development of independence and assertiveness are natural and desirable. Allow them to blossom forth in a healthy environment. If children are not allowed to express themselves in a respectful manner, you can be absolutely certain that they will express themselves in a disrespectful manner, such as resorting to pouting or surly silence.

And incidentally, pouting should be regarded as *intolerable* behavior. It should be dealt with immediately, because it is the most blatant act of nonverbal defiance, next to physical assault, that there is.

b. Our children's assertiveness should not be stifled because they need to have the opportunity to think through with us what our requirements are.

c. They need to learn how to challenge authority respectfully, rationally, reasonably, and deferentially.

d. If you won't listen, someone else will, and the someone else may not provide guidance consistent with your objectives.

e. Last, but far from least, if we've done our job right, our children will have wisdom and insight. They might even give us insight into our own requirements. And we might even have to revise them!

Let us now look at the last **Do not.**

(4)   **Do not** *discuss children's problems when they are within hearing distance.*

Research in education has repeatedly demonstrated that children live up, or down, to a teacher's expectations. In other words, when teachers have been told that normal children were above average or gifted in their ability, and have treated the children accordingly, the children have responded with a level of achievement equal to what the teachers indicated they expected. On the other hand, when teachers treat children as though they are slow, the children respond with lower quality behaviors than they are, in reality, capable of. One fact most educators and counselors are aware of is that the chief cause of many emotional, achievement, or social problems of children is that the children have heard their parents express anxiety, consternation, and dismay over their child's supposed "problems." When the parents' attitudes are changed to reflect optimistic encouragement, in a significant number of cases the problems of their children are greatly diminished.

If you *must* discuss your children when they are within hearing distance, discuss only the positives. Do not discuss their problems.

Avoiding the "Showdown"

In the Old West, the lawmen who lived long and peaceful lives were those who avoided the showdown.

Any western movie in which a confrontation is a part of the plot goes to great lengths to show the patience and sagacity of the tough and grizzled marshal, who courageously avoids, at all costs, the showdown, even though he and the audience both know that he can draw faster, shoot straighter, and survive longer than any of his foolhardy challengers. He will stand victorious, we are shown, amidst the tombstones on boot hill, because he has the courage and the maturity to employ his powers with discretion, because he knows that, in a showdown, even if he survives, he and his community will be hurt.

We and our community--our home--will likewise be hurt in a showdown between us and our children. Yet, many parents do not avoid the showdown, and although they and their children sometimes survive, oftentimes both are seriously wounded, and the harmony of their community, the home, is irreparably damaged.

But how is the showdown avoided? How does a parent avoid the day when the child angrily blurts, "Okay, then I'm leaving!," or the day when the parent's "Or else!" leads to the dreaded sound of a door slammed in finality and the impulsive departure of an irrationally-motivated child? There are two things which can keep a showdown from ever happening.

One element is that of stated expectations, mentioned earlier in this chapter. Remember the list of "Do's" with which this chapter began? If children clearly and unequivocally know what is expected of them, and if they know all the possible consequences which would result from their failure to meet their parents' expectations, there is absolutely no reason for them ever to have a showdown over the consequences. No "Or else's!" or other ultimata are likely to pop up unexpectedly in the heat of anger if the conditions, the expectations, and the consequences of specific behaviors have been outlined, explained, and accepted ahead of time. If the terms of an agreement have been stated and accepted by all parties to the agreement in an atmosphere of love, trust, and tranquillity, then there is no need to negotiate, or even less desirable, to argue, the terms in the heat of high emotions.

There is a second, almost foolproof method of avoiding a showdown, which has been, I believe, a direct answer to my prayers for wisdom in raising my own children, and which has been of incalculable value in handling serious problems in my own home.

When I first read the newspaper account of the story of the prominent citizen's son with which this chapter began, I was horrified to think that a young man, a model of good behavior, would take his own life rather than accept the prospect of facing his disappointed parents. Clearly, his parents had done an extremely good job of impressing a high level of expectations on their son, but they had also created an intolerable burden for him to bear--the burden of perfection, with no room for failure. The son, it was pointed out by friends, had no fear of physical punishment or retribution from his father; nor did he have a fear of losing privileges. His only fear was the humiliation, shame, and guilt over what to him was a grievous and unforgivable offense against his parents.

I had deep empathy for the anguish of this father and mother. They had, without a doubt, succeeded in instilling in their son the same level of expectation of quality behavior I hoped someday to instill in my own children. They had suffered such horrible consequences as a result.

The situation of these well-meaning parents presented an irresolvable dilemma for my wife and me. How could we instill a desire for excellence without imposing the unbearable burden of absolute perfection? How could we convey the idea that, although we might expect excellence, we also anticipated some failures? How could we teach our own children that, although we would admire and praise only their best, we would still love and respect them if they slipped to their worst?

The "Token"

The solution to the problem did not appear at once, as if by magic. Rather, it was the result of much prayer and thinking, but it has never failed in preventing a showdown. It works like this: On the rare occasions in which a child vastly exceeds a parent's highest expectations by behaving in a manner which is clearly extraordinary, the child is given a "token." The token is an uncommon privilege. It is the privilege of avoiding admonishment, criticism, scolding, physical chastening, or the loss of privileges when the child fails to live up to his parents' expectations. In short, the token can be used by a child any time he or she does not want to have to face his parents for doing wrong. The token is redeemable at any time. There are NO exceptions. This last fact is of vital importance, for the purpose of the approach is to allow a child the option of complete safety-- in his mind--

in admitting he did something wrong, without having the incident explicitly mentioned. He or she can admit that something very wrong has been done, without worrying about the humiliation of having the deed discussed or suffering any other parent-imposed consequences.

The token system is absolutely foolproof in avoiding a showdown. It is much more acceptable for a child to avoid a confrontational situation by silently redeeming a token than it is for him to think he has to lie. It is far more tolerable to a child to admit guilt and to admit that he deserves the consequences by silently submitting a token than it is for him to face an outraged or disappointed parent. A situation which could deteriorate into a highly-charged verbal or physical shoving match, or which could result in a slammed door signaling the impulsive independence of a runaway child instead becomes defused by the use of a token. And the end result is desirable: The child has acknowledged the wrongdoing and the fact that he or she needs correction. Self correction, though, rather than parental correction, is the result.

One parent's first use of the token system occurred when his sixteen-year-old son, a strapping six-footer, mowed the lawn and washed the car of a neighbor whose husband had been ill and unable to keep on top of routine tasks. The boy told no one what he had done, but another neighbor had observed his act of kindness and caring. The fact of his outstanding gesture of love had come to his parents' attention in the form of a casual conversation with this neighbor, who complimented the parents, thinking that *they* had directed their son to provide

229

assistance for the sick neighbor. The parents were deeply moved by their son's behavior. They wished to do more than merely commend him, which they did liberally as a matter of habit whenever he carried out his assigned responsibilities around his own home. To offer him money or other privileges as a reward, they wisely concluded, would have demeaned both their son and his act of kindness. Instead, the parents merely told their son, "Kevin, we are extremely pleased with what you did for our neighbor. Your behavior is simply outstanding. The next time you feel that we would be extremely disappointed in you or angry about something you've done, just say, 'I'd like to use the lawn-mowing occasion,' and we will consider the issue closed. You have a token, Kevin, redeemable at any time, which will make it impossible for us to express, with words or actions, our displeasure."

Sure enough, a few weeks later, this same son, the model of responsibility, maturity, and consideration, foolishly participated in a pilfering incident at a local grocery store as a part of a scavenger hunt at a high school initiation ceremony. Although the guilty parties had made restitution and had apologized to the store manager, the principal of the high school nevertheless summoned their parents by letter to appear at the school for a conference. The situation was obviously embarrassing to the parents, who were active in the school, the church, and the community. Their embarrassment was apparent to their son, who himself was ashamed and acutely aware of his parents' unavoidable disappointment. The "showdown," with its accompanying misery for all participants--parents and child alike-- was inevitable. Or was it? As the father later explained:

"Kevin came in after school, mumbled a 'hi' and, head down and eyes averted, started for his room. I said, 'Kevin, I have a letter here from the school, and . . . ' but before I could finish, Kevin said softly, 'Dad, I'd like to use my token.' 'Okay,' I said. And that was all I said. We both knew the issue was resolved. Kevin had acknowledged his error. But what was more important, when he offered and I accepted the token, we were both saying, without words, that we recognized that we all have 'bests' and 'worsts', either of which might emerge at the most unpredictable of times."

Some additional considerations should be kept in mind when the token system is used:

First, a "token" is a *recognition* of an outstanding behavior, not *a reward, or payment,* for the behavior. Consequently, when the token is used by a child to avoid an undesirable confrontation, and when it is accepted by the parent, it is a *recognition* of the fact that we have our "bests," and our "worsts." It is not a payment to make up for the behavior.

Second, tokens should be used, as is the rod, sparingly. My wife and I had given only five tokens to our son by the time he was eighteen years old. Several years later, when he was in his twenties, he remarked that he thought that we were too liberal with our tokens--even though he had used them all! Tokens should be given only for behavior that is truly exceptional in terms of a child's hard work, maturity, responsibility, or Christian love.

Third, to be effective, tokens must be redeemable at any time, *with no exception*. Remember that the sole purpose of the procedure is to provide the child with an open door, no questions asked, out of a potentially humiliating, degrading, or threatening situation which he might go *to any lengths* to avoid, including lying, cheating, talking back, physical assault, running away, or suicide. If there are to be exceptions to the use of a token by a child, specify them in advance. But to be effective in providing complete safety in the child's mind, there should be no exceptions.

The token system, as indicated previously, has been one of the most invaluable assets imaginable in administering a program of discipline which is designed to be inspirational, constructive, and positive. As Christians, we are aware that, because of Jesus Christ, God in His grace does not always allow us to suffer the consequences of our failure to attain perfect obedience to Him. He provides, instead, the conditions in which *"A just man falleth seven times and riseth up again,"* and we pray, with the Psalmist, that, *"If Thou, Lord, shouldest mark iniquities, Lord who shall stand?"* As Christian parents, we can do no less than provide the same positive conditions for constructive growth, taking care to point out to our children that our patience with them and our love for them are a direct outgrowth of the love of Christ for us, and that our acceptance of them is not dependent upon their trading in a token. A Scripture which would be a most appropriate reference to share with children on this subject would be Romans 3:27,28 (TLB), which says:

> *Then what can we boast about doing, to earn our salvation? Nothing at all, Why? Because our*

232

acquittal is not based on our good deeds; it is based on what Christ has done and our faith in Him.

So it is that we are saved by faith in Christ and not by the good things we do.

Summary

There is only one major goal of discipline by Christian parents: faith in Jesus Christ and life everlasting for their children. All aspects of a child's training are directed toward attaining this goal. Discipline, therefore, is always positive. Discipline is always training. Undesirable behaviors, in view of this fact, are regarded as behaviors which must be changed or corrected in order that the child might be able to more directly set his sights on those behaviors, attitudes, and values which lead to growth in faith in Jesus Christ. Since discipline is training, it is important to remember that even the best-trained individuals in any field of endeavor experience failure from time to time, and that they must have the opportunity to try again. Giving a child a second chance or many chances to improve and correct his behavior, then, is entirely consistent with good discipline.

In addition to the scriptural admonitions to teach children the Word of God, God has provided parents with the opportunity to learn from their own experiences and from the experiences of others in administering discipline. There are some practical "do's" and "do not's" which parents and teachers have discovered to be useful as guidelines in administering discipline, including how to avoid the showdown" and its destructive effects.

Chapter Twelve

"Promises, Promises"

"Promises, promises." We've all heard this expression. Sometimes, it is used sarcastically in regard to someone's stated intentions. Often, it's a skeptical and caustic prediction that no real results are to be expected--only empty words. Frequently, it's a bitterly cynical expression of disappointment as a result of someone's failure to keep his word.

For the Christian parent who earnestly desires to follow God's commandments in discipline, however, the expression takes on an entirely new and thrilling meaning. "Promises, promises!" the Christian parent can confidently and triumphantly declare. We optimistically exult in the certain fact that those who place their faith and confidence in the promises of the Eternal God--the Ancient of Days--will never be disappointed.

In my professional life, as I frequently try to solve problems caused by the spiritual carnage wreaked upon unsuspecting young people by a rapidly changing and increasingly threatening materialistic world, it has become alarmingly evident to me that deep spiritual wisdom is critical in successfully raising children. Philosophically appealing psychological theories don't work. Child-rearing strategies concocted in the minds of even brilliant human beings don't work. They can't prevail against what the Scripture calls "the fiery darts of the wicked." *Wisdom*, not brilliance and insight, is needed. *Wisdom*, not human reason and philosophical profundity, is all that will prevail.

But where do parents find wisdom? How do they even *begin* to acquire wisdom? Some of the richest people in the world have spent thousands of dollars searching for some magical psychological, pharmacological, or metaphysical cure that can mend broken lives and twisted minds. Deep regret is often all that is left of parents' dreams for their children's future, because parents listened to "modern" and "accepted" theories of child-rearing which totally ignored the wisdom provided by God in His Word.

Only in the Word of God can the kind of wisdom be found to construct a spiritual fortress that can withstand the fierce and unrelenting assault on the minds and souls of our children. God has told us where to find wisdom. We can take the *first* step and the *only* step which can be taken in seeking wisdom by acting upon God's declaration. God says:

> *The fear of the Lord is the beginning of wisdom; knowledge of the Holy One is understanding.* (Proverbs 9:10) (AAT)

And as we grow in our knowledge of God and in the fear of the Lord, we can nurture and train our children with the steadfast and firm assurance that, no matter what happens, we do not need to be afraid or anxious about our children, for God also says:

> *In fearing the Lord you can have confidence and strength, and your children will have security. (Proverbs 14:26).(AAT)*

The security provided for our children is unassailable. Nothing can weaken it, defeat it, or destroy it, for it is guaranteed by God Himself.

It is for these two reasons--the first, that wisdom and insight are always the result of growth in the knowledge of God, and the second, that growth in the knowledge and fear of God provide a refuge for my children, that I am firmly and unequivocally committed to the program of discipline outlined in this book, for the program of discipline is nothing more than the natural outcome of the commandment in Deuteronomy 6:6-8:

> *These words which I command you this day shall be upon your heart; and you shall teach them diligently to your children, and shall talk of them when you sit in your house, and when you walk by the way, and when you lie down, and when you rise.*

And when, with the help of the Holy Spirit, I follow this commandment, my children will grow in the Lord. And my children will be led to say:

> How I love Your teaching--I think about it all day long.
> Because I always have Your commandments, I'm wiser than my enemies.
> I have a better insight than all my teachers because I think of the truths You wrote.
> I understand better than the old men because I follow the way You want me to live.
> I keep my foot from walking on any evil path--
> I want to do what You say.
> I haven't turned away from your precepts because you have taught me . . .
> Your Word is a lamp for my feet and a light on my path.
> (Psalm 119:97-102; 105, 106) (AAT)

Your children's growth in the knowledge of God provides multiple benefits. In the Book of Proverbs God outlines desirable behaviors for His people, He promises His blessings upon those who obey His commandments, and He describes what you can confidently expect for your children when they learn according to God's commandment. God says, in Proverbs 2:1, 5-12, and 3:2,4:

> My child, if you receive my words and treasure up my commandments with you . . .

*Then you will understand the fear of the Lord
and find the knowledge of God. For the Lord gives
wisdom;
from His mouth come knowledge and
understanding He is a shield to those who walk in
integrity,
Guarding the paths of justice and preserving the
way of His saints. Then you will understand
righteousness and justice and equity, every good
path;
for wisdom will come into your heart,
and knowledge will be pleasant to your soul;*

*Discretion will watch over you; Understanding will
guard you;
Delivering you from the way of evil. . . .*

*Length of days and years of life and abundant
welfare will they give you.*

*So you will find favor and good repute in the sight
of God and man.*

Consider this: Your obedience to God in doing what
is the *bare minimum* required by God can produce the
kind of person described above--a person of wisdom,
integrity, knowledge, and understanding and discretion--a
person who enjoys an outstanding reputation among
other people, and who is the beneficiary of God's favor.
But the fantastic blessings above, which result from the
training you provide for your children according to God's
commandment, are only a minor part of the success

which you as a Christian parent can expect. For God provides an even greater source of peace of mind for us if we lead our children to faith in Jesus Christ. Regardless of what lies in the future for my children, I can promise them, with secure, serene, and triumphant confidence, what the Apostle Paul declared in the eighth chapter of his letter to the Christians in Rome:

> *I'm convinced that no death or life, no angels or their rulers, nothing now or in the future, no powers, nothing above or below, or any other creature can ever separate us from God, who loves us in Christ Jesus, our Lord.* (Rom. 8:38,39) (AAT)

This, then, is my confidence. *My discipline cannot fail.* I have "*trained up my child in The Way he should go, and when he is old, he will not depart from it*".

The Way, is Jesus. The Truth is Jesus. And the Life is Jesus.

The Way he should go is the way of Jesus Christ, the Son of God.

Appendix A
Scripture Texts for Spiritual Survival

The Bible verses listed in this section are an immediate, first-line defense for our children. Verses were selected which our kids could use to respond to challenges posed by anti-Christian philosophies, by rampant materialism, by adversity, and by self-doubt, anxiety, and stress. When committed to memory, these verses will help our children survive spiritually. They will be a clear, dependable, certain, and unchanging foundation--a solid rock upon which our children can build their lives.

Throughout this book, in some instances I have presented verses using *TheLiving Bible,* in other instances, Albert Beck's *An American Translation,* and in still other instances, the *King James Version.* In each instance in which a particular version of the Scripture was chosen, the choice was based upon which version would provide the clearest meaning without violating accuracy. I've found that it is extremely important to constantly teach young people to apply the Word--something they can't do if they don't understand it.

Analysis of the *Living Bible* through the use of a readability formula--a method of determining the school grade level or reading difficulty level of printed material--reveals that the *Living New Testament* is written at about a sixth grade level. It is often the version which is easiest for parents to explain. However, if the King James version is the only version you trust, use it with confidence, and explain it the best you can. You'll be surprised at how much your children will assimilate.

What If Children Don't Understand Certain Verses?

It should be pointed out, that, as is sometimes the case with adults, we can expect that full understanding of some verses may not be immediately attained by a child. If that's the case, parents should choose whichever version of the Scriptures they are most comfortable with. The important thing to remember is to both explain the *meaning* of each verse, and to identify for the child *why* the verse is important to know.

If full understanding doesn't take place immediately, don't let it deter you from helping your children to memorize Scripture. To be sure, it's highly *desirable* for young children to have a clear understanding of each verse as it is memorized. But it is *not necessary* that each verse be fully understood as it is committed to memory. For example, I've done surveys with adults and college students in which they were asked to identify inspirational quotations which were meaningful to them. A significant number of respondents indicated that, at the time they memorized some inspirational reference, they did not fully understand it. In some cases, they reported that it was not until years later that "a light went on", and they finally "got it."

As you work with your children, it will be necessary to explain the Scriptures, and then re-explain them, and, perhaps, re-explain them again. But don't be surprised if your children come up with a new dimension of understanding of a Scripture reference. It might even be a perspective that you hadn't thought of when you first explained it to them!

242

SCRIPTURES RELATING TO SALVATION

(RIGHTEOUSNESS)

John 3:16	KIV	Acts 4:12	KJV
Acts 16:30	KJV	Romans 3:21, 22.27	LNT
John 11:25	KJV	Ephesians 2:8,9	KJV
John 14:6	KJV	Galatians 3:6	KJV
John 5:24	LNT	Philippians 3:9	LNT
Proverbs 14:12	KJV	Philippians 1:6	KJV
Proverbs 22:6	KJV		

SCRIPTURES RELATING TO ANXIETY

(RECOVERY)

Philippians 4:13	KJV	Romans 8:28	KJV
Proverbs 29:26	RSV	Romans 8:38	KJV
Romans 5:3-5	LNT	Proverbs 3:5,6	KJV
2 Timothy 2:13	LNT	Philippians 4:6,7	LNT
Matthew 6:31-34	KJV	Matthew 10:28-31	LNT

SCRIPTURES RELATING TO HOW TO LIVE

(RELATIONSHIPS AND RESISTANCE)

Matthew 5:13, 15, 16	LNT	John 15:5	KJV
Matthew 5:39, 40, 41	LNT	Romans 12:2	LNT
Matthew 16:24-26	LNT	Colossians 3:17	LNT
Hebrews 11:6	LNT	2 Timothy 4:3,4	LNT
2 Timothy 2:16	LNT	Ephesians 6:11,12	KJV

APPENDIX B

Some Additional Thoughts
On Proverbs 22:6

Some students of Christian discipline perceive a problem in drawing inferences on Christian training from Proverbs 22:6. Their difficulty has been encountered in working with a translation of the verse which approximates, as closely as possible, the literal Hebrew, which yields two facets of the verse which differ from the traditionally accepted King James translation. Specifically, it has been asserted that the literal Hebrew translation instructs us to train a child "according to his way"; i.e., that, since the noun "way" carries the masculine singular suffix, the word "way" indicates that the emphasis of the verse is on training appropriate to the child's developmental level, rather than on a readily identifiable body of content, which has been the traditional interpretation, and which is the interpretation of the author.

The author interprets "way" as being ultimately indicative of a body of content because this conclusion appears readily tenable even if "way" is interpreted in the literal sense. Even if it is acknowledged that the literal translation of the Hebrew text is an admonishment to us to train a child "according to what is appropriate for a given level" (and certainly training which is not appropriate in the "how" or which is not cognizant of an appropriate level will, without doubt, fail) the author's position is that one conclusion is inescapable.

The "training" identified in Proverbs 22:6 could not conceivably be training in occupational skills--such training would be inconsistent with the child's needs, abilities, and so on, thereby missing the intent of the Scripture text. The training could also not be training in social skills, for even though a body of content in social skills could probably be identified for a given developmental level, it is not likely that social skills appropriate for a given society or a given age level would be appropriate in a different society or at a different age level. The desirability of perseverance of social skills, then, would be questionable. Similar arguments could be raised concerning "coping" abilities or "emotional survival" skills taught without reference to the teachings of Scripture, which show us how to cope successfully because we stand on the Rock; that is, on the teaching of Jesus Christ.

In the author's judgment, then, there are two factors in Proverbs 22:6 which are of deep concern to parents and teachers. The first is that training should be appropriate for the child's needs, abilities, or whatever. The second is that training should embody content which is unquestionably desirable as a lifelong possession; i.e., the content of the Scriptures, or spiritual training. There is simply no other content which would, on close examination, be valid at any age level and in any set of conditions. Certainly, occupational content, social skills content, or any other content would not necessarily be applicable to all situations, all societies, and in all phases of life.

A second issue which might pose a problem for some students of Christian discipline also relates to the literal Hebrew. It has been asserted that the Hebrew conjunction probably should be translated as "even," rather than "and," as the King James Version renders it. In addressing this point, the author concludes that the translation "even" would serve to support the major emphasis of the book even more tenably than the translation of the conjunction as "and," since the only appropriate definition or interpretation of "even" in this case would be the phrase "in spite of." This interpretation--"in spite of"--implies an adverse condition, or, at least, a condition not conducive to the continuance or perseverance of the behaviors which preceded it. That is, "and" implies a smooth transition from point "A," "training," to point "B," persistence of training over an extended period of time. "Even" implies not only persistence of training over an extended period of time, but perseverance in conditions which are adverse or inimical to the initial behavior. Moses' behavior as an adult in Egypt is an outstanding example of the persistence of his early training by his mother in the face of conditions inimical to the values he was taught. The Scriptures tell us that, "It was by faith that Moses, when he grew up, refused to be treated as the grandson of the King, but chose to share ill-treatment with God's people instead of enjoying the fleeting pleasures of sin" (Hebrews 11:24,25).

About one thing in Proverbs 22:6, however, there is no disagreement. God both admonishes us and encourages us to provide God directed discipline for our children.

Appendix C

Answers to A Quiz on the Four Rs (pages 125-130)

Below are brief explanations of what each item in the "Quiz" represents, along with Scripture verses that apply to each item. Your children will be challenged by many such statements as they make their way through life. The statements in the quiz are those commonly heard, in one form or another, on the campus and in the workplace.

Quiz Items, Explanations, and Scripture References

1. The statement in this item challenges the idea that Jesus is the only way to heaven, and promotes the idea that everybody is going to heaven, as long as they are "sincere" and "try to be good." Close to that notion is the idea that "God" is known by different names, regardless of whether we call Him "Jesus", "The Great Spirit", "Allah", and so on. These ideas are rebutted by John 14:6; John 3:14-18; John 3:36; I John 5:12; I Timothy 2:5,6.
    The statement in this item represents the most serious challenge to your child's wellbeing that he or she will ever encounter, so it's crucial that a child be able to respond with Scripture. If we try to argue the question logically, we will not be able to, because the Christian idea of salvation is not "logical" to an unsaved person. In fact, the Bible says that the unsaved person will regard it as "foolishness." (I Corinthians 1: 18-25; and I Corinthians 2:14).

2. This item promotes the familiar argument that people who are "good guys" will go to heaven because they are "good", meaning, simply, that "good deeds" or "good works" are what save us. The best response to this argument—which sounds logical, but which is not supported by the Bible, is Ephesians 2: 8-10. In this verse, Paul says that it is *grace*—that is, God's undeserved kindness—which saves us when we have faith in Christ. The verse goes on to say that it is a *gift* of God, not a result of good works, *"just in case anybody wants to brag about it."* This verse can stand alone to rebut the "good deeds" argument. John 6:28 and 29 are also two very powerful verses: they are Jesus' direct answer to the question, *"What are the works [good deeds] God wants us to do?"*
    One thing we should take note of, here, is that it's easy to get sidetracked and start arguing about whether you can be saved without doing any good works, and so on. In fact, there are different ideas in various denominations about whether good works are essential, whether they are important, how important they are, and on and on. That's not the point of this item in the quiz. This item in the quiz reflects the popular notion that works *alone*, without faith in Christ, will earn a person's way into heaven. And regardless of where you stand on the place of good works in the life of a believer, what is essential to know is that *without faith in Christ, salvation is impossible*, irrespective of whether the person is the greatest performer of good works the

246

world has ever seen. Galatians 2:21, provides additional clarification on the issue. So does Titus 3:5.

3. This comment has been used to justify everything from abortion to homosexual marriage to premarital sex to so-called "justifiable adultery" when one partner is unable or unwilling to have sex. It embodies the popular myth that God is "the Man Upstairs" who winks at our sins, and that what is sin in one era of history might not be a sin in another era. People who argue this position are fond of citing the ceremonial laws in the Old Testament, and saying, "Well, then, why don't we punish people for _____
_____ (fill in the blank, because here they come up with the most ridiculous example they can think of)". Again, the best answer is an answer that is Scripture, rather than to try to argue from human intelligence. In the Bible, Jesus answers the argument quite directly in Matthew 5:18, and in Luke 16:17. Further, in I Corinthians chapter 5, there is a lengthy discussion of sexual sin, which Chapter 7 clarifies as any sexual activity occurring outside of marriage. I Corinthians 6: 9-20 provides additional insight, and II Peter Chapter 2 also discusses the topic, as does II Timothy 2:22.

4. Romans 6: 1,2 is the best response to this item.

5. This item is a challenge to the concept of "original sin," which teaches that, except for Jesus Christ, all people are born as sinners. It would pay to check your church's position on this concept. (Some churches teach that there is an "age of accountability", whereas other churches teach that a newborn baby is sinful.) The author's perspective is that all people are born as sinners, and, therefore, they need a Savior. One Scripture verse he refers to in support of this idea is Psalm 51:5. Romans 5:12-21 has been used to present a broad perspective: the teaching that all human beings are under the curse of sin, whether or not they have had the opportunity to choose to sin or to choose not to sin.

6. There is a false teaching that health and wealth are sure to follow belief in Christ. It's closely related to another false idea: that God wants us to be happy. Neither of these ideas is supported by Scripture. God wants us to have joy, but "joy" and "happiness" are not necessarily the same thing. I Peter 4:19 tells us that, in fact, God may want us to suffer in certain instances. Colossians I: 11,12, talks about "enduring patiently" in the same breath as Paul talks about "joyfully thanking" the Father. Finally, the verses listed in item #3, above, can be used to show that we should not live the way unsaved people live, and Colossians Chapter 3 also includes verses that pertain to this item.

7. Mark 10:9. Matthew 5:31,32. Also, I Corinthians 7:12-16 sheds additional light on the subject. Traditionally, the Christian church has recognized only unfaithfulness as legitimate grounds for divorce, and makes no provision for divorce because people have "fallen out of love", or because they have fallen for somebody else besides their spouse, or because they "don't get along."

247

8. Many verses can be used to respond to this item, but one that is commonly cited is Matthew 10:29-31. The smallest unit that people of Jesus' time could comprehend was probably "the hairs of your head." Today, Jesus might say, "Even your DNA is written down in God's book, so don't worry, because God is in charge of every detail of your life." Psalm 46: 1-3; Luke 12:5; Proverbs 3:25, and many other verses also apply. A good Concordance will provide many references under "fear", "afraid", and so on, and verses of varying levels of difficulty for children of different ages can be readily found.

9. See above.

10. See above.

11. See above. Luke 6: 47,48 promises Christians that if they follow the teachings of Jesus, when calamity comes, they will be able to weather the storms of life. In Matthew 6: 34, Jesus tells Christians not to worry about tomorrow. (See Luke 12:22-32 for a discussion about worry.)

12. Matthew 28: 19,20 is probably the best response to the argument asserted in #12. In America and Canada especially, the idea that you shouldn't try to "foist off" your beliefs on somebody else is regarded as a virtue. So Christians are criticized when they try to share the gospel, even though society says it's okay to push beliefs about homosexuality, "safe" sex, and just about anything else. Unfortunately, many Christians have swallowed the lie that "religion is a private matter", and they've failed to follow Matthew 28: 19 and 20, which is referred to as *The Great Commission*. We think that we are supposed to "mind our own business", and we don't realize that it *is* our business to witness to other people. In fact, it's our *chief* business as disciples of Jesus Christ! (Matthew 5:13-16).

13. Christians are called "narrow minded" primarily when they make the statement that Jesus is the only way to heaven. There is no logical argument that is acceptable to people who are not believers, but the criticism is such a stinging attack that our kids often recoil from it as though they had been bitten by a snake. The only satisfactory response to the "narrow minded" accusation is one that we can use to remind *ourselves*—not others—of why we believe in a "narrow-minded" way: Matthew 7:14. All of the verses that can be used in item #1, above, also apply. But, all things considered, the accusation is true. We *are* "narrow-minded." Thank God for that blessing! (By the way, Jesus was "narrow-minded." Imagine, saying that He, Himself, was the only way to heaven!)

14. The argument in this item is a variation of the argument Satan used with Jesus when he tried to tempt Jesus to jump off the pinnacle of the temple. Jesus' words in Matthew 4:7 give us a proper perspective on the issue. It's true that God protects us in all situations, but we are very clearly told not to "tempt the Lord our God."

15. II Corinthians 11: 23-33 is an account of Paul's terrible suffering as he obeyed God in preaching the Gospel. If trouble could be avoided by being "obedient", then we could mistakenly conclude that Paul must have seriously disobeyed God. As far as that goes, we could draw the same erroneous conclusion about Jesus! There are many other verses that teach that trouble is a normal part of life, even for obedient Christians. The first part of Romans 5 would be a good reference to look at. Hebrews 10: 32-36, and Hebrews 12: 7-13 also apply. James 1:2-4 would also be good verses to commit to memory, as well as I Peter 4: 12-19. And then, there's John 16:32, in which Jesus tells us that we will have trouble, and there's also the verse that tells us that "all who desire to lead a godly life in Christ Jesus will be persecuted. (II Timothy 3:12).

16. James, in his epistle, talks about why people don't get what they ask for. (James 4: 2,3). These verses alone are a sufficient argument to refute the idea that God is some kind of a genie who provides instant gratification when we want "things." There are too many verses on prayer to list here, but if a careful study is made of prayer, it will quickly be seen that God does not promise to satisfy our every whim that we bring forth in prayer. Even Jesus prayed, "Father, if you are willing . . ."

17. Although the statement is true, because God certainly does not restrict Himself to being discovered only in formal worship services or in organized Bible studies, in Hebrews 10:25, Christians are admonished not to forsake "the assembling of themselves together." In other words, we can't argue—at least, not with support from the Bible—that we don't need to get together with other Christians. That would be a direct violation of the admonition in verse 25 of Hebrews 10. On the other hand, it's harder to argue that the verse means that you have to go to church, or to formal services. In fact, in Colossians 2: 16-23, there's quite a lengthy discussion about Christian freedom, and about rules, regulations, religious practices, holy days, and other such things. Now, in view of all of these verses, it's safe to say that Christians are not supposed to neglect getting together with other Christians. And it's clear that what is meant is that, during those "get-togethers", the focus is on doing things that are "Christian". That could be worship, Bible study, and other faith-strengthening activities. Bottom line, then? God did not intend for Christians to "go it alone." He directs us to get together.

18. The references in Corinthians, at the end of item #1, apply here. But an argument that is often overlooked is that Jesus, Himself, referred to Noah and The Flood. He also referred to Jonah and Jonah's being swallowed by a huge sea creature. Some liberal theologians argue that Jesus was simply "adapting Himself to an error of His times", and that He, Himself, knew that the Creation stories and The Flood stories were merely myths. If we accept that argument, we would have to conclude that Jesus knowingly participated in promoting error. That, in turn, would violate the Bible verse that says, "He never sinned or was found to be deceiving when He spoke." (I Peter 2:22).

19. See above.

20. Matthew 7:6. Proverbs 26:4,5. The author recommends that students not engage their professors in debate, in public, over matters of faith. The author also recommends that, before our kids engage professors or teachers in a private discussion of faith, they attempt to discern whether the person hearing the Christian message is disdainful of it, or open to it. In most cases, professors who have made a career out of "shredding" Christian values will verbally destroy immature Christian kids, and nothing is to be gained by debating theological points.

On the other hand, Christian kids should be encouraged to stand up for their beliefs if they are being unfairly attacked. In other words, they should not always try to argue the validity of their beliefs. But they should be encouraged to argue the validity of their right to hold Christian beliefs. The Proverbs references mean, simply, that foolish arguments, asserted by fools, should not be dignified by an earnest response. At the same time, foolish arguments which could be lent credence by other listeners simply by being unchallenged, should be rebutted with vigor and confidence. Great discernment is needed on the part of Christian kids, especially on the university campus.

21. Here, we need verses that pertain to God's control of situations that affect us. The story of Joseph, and especially Genesis 50:20, is a wonderful example of how God will take the evil intentions of others and make them work for our good. The whole narrative in the Book of Esther is another wonderful story of how God "turns the tables" on people who try to hurt believers. Finally, there are many references in the Psalms that pertain, even, to those who try to hurt us with harmful gossip, or slander. Here, also, Romans 8:28 applies when we fear are verses that apply to worrying about unanticipated catastrophe or tragedy.

22. The statement in this item can, on close examination, be used to justify just about anything short of murder. It's a variation of the "I can do anything I want to; I'm saved by grace." It's also a variation of the "times have changed" argument. Several verses are appropriate in response to this argument: Romans 12:2, applies. (The Living Bible version is easiest for young children to understand). I Corinthians 10:31 is a verse that applies to this item, as well as to a whole array of things Christians might think are just fine for them to do: "Whether you eat or drink or do anything else, do everything to glorify God." That's a pretty simple test that any person can apply to his or her own conscience. Finally, the verses below can be useful to remind a Christian of what to be aware of concerning entertainment, teachings we listen to, and so on: I Corinthians 5: 6-12; Galatians 5:9; Matthew 16:6, 11,12; Mark 8:15; Luke 12:1. (All of these verses warn us about the danger of "just a little bit" of exposure to harmful influences).

23. There are a lot of so-called "New Age" approaches to finding wisdom. Dabbling in the supernatural is one of them. The Bible clearly teaches that Christians are to find their wisdom and insight in the Word of God. Deuteronomy 18:10 is perhaps the strongest Biblical prohibition against

playing with the supernatural. It expressly forbids Christians from using devices like seances, psychics, and other "supernatural" channels. Some references that also apply are Acts 16:16-20, where a young woman who actually told the truth under the influence of a demonic spirit had the spirit cast out of her by Paul. Galatians 5:20 refers to witchcraft (which would include all psychic phenomena depended upon for guidance) as a sin. So does I Samuel 15:23. Exodus 22:18 also refers to psychic phenomena. God promises to guide us and to lead us; therefore, He wants us to turn to Him, not psychic phenomena, for guidance.

24. Whenever God's forgiveness is being discussed, one thing is more common than hearing the name of Jeffrey Dahmer, the infamous murderer who not only killed people, but also cannibalized them. It's more common to hear the name of the worst criminal one can think of at the time God's grace is being discussed. The criminal's name is then followed by a statement such as, "If God lets somebody like that into heaven, that's not a heaven where I want to go." What the statement represents, when it is closely analyzed, is a philosophy of "works" righteousness. It's just a variation of the idea that some things are just too bad to ever be forgiven, and that, after all is said and done, there has to be at least some good in a person if the person is to get into heaven. Children who know the story of the thief on the cross will be able to cite his salvation as an example of God's grace: after all, the thief on the cross didn't have a chance to get down off the cross and live a life to "redeem himself." The example of St. Paul can also be used to show that God forgives the worst of sins. (Galatians 1:13: Paul persecuted Christians and tried to destroy the church). And if you really think about it, what sin could be worse than the sin of murdering the Son of God? Nevertheless, Jesus prayed, "Father forgive them," for the very people who were in the act of murdering Him and mocking Him!

25. Romantic heartbreak might be something that we adults don't take too seriously. However, young people have committed suicide over receiving a "Dear John" or "Dear Jane" letter. Some young people have gone off the deep end in other ways, requiring hospitalization or psychiatric care, while others have committed murder of the person who jilted them, or of the person they perceived to be responsible for their breakup. Verses such as Romans 8:28, Proverbs 3:5,6, (or Proverbs 19:14, especially) can help your child overcome the heartache of romantic trauma. Any verse that would fit in items #9 and 10, above, would also fit.

Summary:

The Bible teaches that "all these things" in the Bible were written for our instruction, so that we might have hope. If we can meet any challenge of life with the power of God's Word to keep us encouraged and comforted, we can't possibly fail. Not only that, but we can be a source of comfort and encouragement to others, and help them bear the burdens of life. It's pretty easy to see that teaching our children to memorize God's Word is the most wonderful gift we can ever give them.